The
Begrudger's
Guide to
Irish Politics
Breandán Ó hEithir

POOLBEG

A Paperback Original
First published 1986 by
Poolbeg Press Ltd,
Knocksedan House,
Swords, Co. Dublin, Ireland.

Reprinted 1986
Reprinted 1987

© Breandán O hEithir 1986

ISBN 0 905169 74 3

Cover illustration by Martyn Turner
Design by Steven Hope
Photoset by Wellset Ltd.,
48 Hardwicke Street, Dublin 1.
Printed by the Guernsey Press Co. Ltd.,
Guernsey, Channel Islands.

This book is dedicated to those
who still believe that the island of Ireland
has a foreseeable political future.

Contents

Foreword

"We will in our arse have our own gentry"

The morning after the Anglo-Irish Treaty of 1921 was signed in London, the parish priest of a small parish in West Cork was returning home from church, after mass, reading the *Cork Examiner*. It was a great day for Ireland and no doubt about it. Mick Collins and the boys had pulled it off. Old Ireland was free at last.

He exorcised the last lingering memories of the sermons he had preached in the recent past, excommunicating them by bell, book and candle as the double-dyed murderers of the legal forces of law and order — Irishmen too as often as not — as well as innocent civilians. Well, this put paid to the anti-God forces of Communism at any rate! The parish priest set his features in an ecstatic smile.

Then, out of the corner of his eye, he saw the village blacksmith walking slowly up the opposite side of the street to his forge.

"Good morning, Con. A great day for Ireland, thank God!"

"Good morning, Father," muttered the blacksmith, without any enthusiasm whatever. "I suppose it's a great day for some."

"Oh, come, come, my good man! Cheer up and celebrate Ireland's freedom. The best days are yet to come."

"Not for me they aren't, Father. It was the gentry kept me going and what's left of them are going to leave the country now. Ireland may be free but I'm ruined."

1

"Now Con, my dear man, will you listen to your parish priest. Everything will be all right. We're going to have our own gentry now. Believe you me."

And with these honeyed words of hope the parish priest sailed off to his breakfast. The blacksmith shook his head slowly and silently, but as he turned to go he was clearly heard to mutter,

"Our own gentry! We will in our arse have our own gentry."

The blacksmith, whose name did not survive in the folk memory, has the distinction of being the first recorded Irish begrudger under the freedom to achieve freedom which the Treaty gave to twenty-six of the thirty-two counties, according to some of its signatories.

His simple utterance sums up the fundamental attitude of that most numerous section of Irish society. It is a deep and abiding doubt about our ability to run our own affairs as well as others might run them for us. Our country, the manner in which it is run and those who run it, are a source of deep and constant disappointment to the begrudger.

Even the most idiotic of Irish politicians would have to admit that the country has not actually flourished since independence was granted to us, sixty-five years ago. It would have to be admitted that the begrudgers in our midst have increased mightily and filled the land with their plaintive cries and lamentations. Pubs, radio chat shows, the correspondence columns of newspapers, the very air of the country is full of their constant crises of confidence, their unshakable faith in matters always turning out to be much worse than expected, their uncanny ability to detect feet of clay that extend to the armpit and beyond. . . .

Still, the begrudger is not a thoroughly bad fellow in all respects, despite being cast into the bilges of our society (by hob-philosophers as well as the radio and television variety, who like to blame the begrudger for all our ills) with the phrase, "Fuck the begrudgers"; or more genteel and socially acceptable variations on that same theme.

It is a little unfair. The begrudger is one whose keen

realism has triumphed over his idealism and brought him into direct conflict with received wisdom. It is true that he makes up for his lack of conventional faith by a rather unscrupulous use of odd facts, frequently stood on their heads. It must be confessed also that his stock in trade consists of slur, innuendo and guilt by association; a fault he shares with some contemporary historians, politicians and, more particularly, with those who market politicians through the media, for consumption by the public.

Still, only in rare instances does the Irish begrudger lack the virtue of bluntness. If, for instance, he chooses to adopt a certain attitude to the "unfortunate division of this green and pleasant isle", he will not consider it necessary to weave intricate scenarios around his thoughts, or conceal his poisoned barbs in the profusion of polished periods.

He will merely say, "Fuck the Catholics anyway! Let them like it or lump it."

This healthy, if somewhat uncomfortable attitude, would also extend to affairs and issues far removed from the surrounding cabbage-patch. Taking a lingering look at that other trouble-spot, the Middle-East, our begrudger would cut any possible tedious thesis short and come straight to the point: "The Israelis have possession, and the means need not bother us at this stage. They have the best army and the backing of the right super-power. They even revived their auld language, which is more than can be said for others not a million miles from us. So bugger the Arabs, it's their hard luck!"

The begrudger has been described as having a grass-hopper mind cursed with an elephant's memory. Be that as it may, he is a truly Irish phenomenon, as the term is scarcely known in the rest of the English-speaking world. He tries hard not to bore, which is why his attention is constantly attracted to new subjects and to the dissection of new paragons of probity.

And his reaction to current events is not always predictable. On a recent occasion, when the Modern History Department of University College Dublin (which my informant described as a Confraternity of Latter-Day Blueshirts) became involved publicly in what is usually called "The Revision of Irish History", a registered begrudger of my acquaintance gave me a ballad which he had composed to mark the occasion.

It seems that a well-intentioned, but rather inexperienced, member of the department wrote to a committee in Southwark, in London, taking them to task for dedicating a series of public lectures on Irish history to the memory of Terence MacSwiney. The UCD Modern History Department, said the letter, would certainly not contribute to an event calculated to give aid and comfort to subversives and other perverts who, like MacSwiney, presumably believe that it is those who suffer most rather than those who inflict most who will conquer. However, a member of the department did give a lecture in Southwark, which goes to show that even in the Modern History Department of UCD, shades of green may be detected among the blue.

This was but one of the conclusions my begrudger friend came to. Another concerned the complete absence of anything that could be classified as a revisionist ballad. He maintained that to succeed with the public at large, and particularly with the younger generation (who are still taught a lot of conventional modern history, despite the commendable efforts of people like the fledgling scholar in UCD who is clearly marked for greatness), one has to break into the charts with the message.

This ballad, which is but a modest effort in a good cause, tries to put a more human face on a force that got more than its share of bad publicity: the Black and Tans. It does have the virtue of utter simplicity and the events mentioned should be known to most primary school pupils. It may be sung to a wide variety of melancholy airs, such as "The Rocks of Bawn". However, should a singer have qualms about marrying the words to a reputable tune it is possible to sing it very rapidly to the air of the double-jig, "Coinnigh do Thóin leis na Driseacha".

4

The Gentle Black and Tan

Come all you staunch revisionists
And listen to my song,
It's short and it's unusual
And it won't detain you long.
It's all about a soldier
Who has carried history's can,
Who dodged Tom Barry and Dan Breen
The gentle Black and Tan.

'Twas the curse of unemployment
That drove him to our shore.
His jacket black and trousers tan
Like a badge of shame he wore.
"Subdue the rebel Irish
And shoot them when you can!"
"May God forgive me if I do,"
Prayed the gentle Black and Tan.

The burning of Cork City
Was indeed a mighty blaze.
The jewellers' shops were gutted
Not before the spoils were shared.
Gold and silver ornaments,
Rings and watches for each man,
"But I only struck the matches,"
Said the gentle Black and Tan.

Croke Park on Bloody Sunday
Was our hero's greatest test.
The spectators on the terraces
Nigh impossible to miss.
With salt tears his eyes were blinded
And down his cheeks they ran,
So he only shot Mick Hogan
The gentle Black and Tan.

So take heed you blinkered Nationalists
Fair warning take from me.
If you want to live in safety
And keep this land at sea.
Take heed of our three heroes
Murphy, Edwards and Yer Man,
Who will sing the fame and clear the name
Of the gentle Black and Tan.

Before we leave the stage to the central character it is as well to point out that occasionally — very rarely in recent times, it must be said — a begrudger leaves his stool at the bar counter and manages to gain a seat in Dáil Eireann. Here too he will be easily identified by the simplicity and the straightforward nature of his utterances.

For our present purposes one example will have to suffice. The speaker came from the south of Ireland, and is no longer in the land of the living, and the debate concerned the low price his constituents were getting for their sugar beet.

That foreign sugar was imported at £12 a ton higher than the price of the best white sugar leaving our own factory. When I saw the imports and the price, I went to the then General Manager of the Sugar Company, General Costello, and I said, "We never fought in this country to have a foreign nigger getting £12 a ton more for his sugar than an Irish farmer."

With the begrudger you always know where you stand, even though his own stances may change with baffling rapidity. What follows is his selective run through aspects of Irish politics since the signing of that Treaty, and particularly the troubles that followed; troubles that seem to be increasing even as we pen these words.

1

"Early this morning
I signed my death warrant"

In the beginning — for this is where we have chosen to begin — there was unity of purpose and what Eamon de Valera, during the Treaty debate in Dáil Eireann, called "the magnificent discipline" of what became known as the Four Glorious Years. Then came a truce, peace negotiations, a Treaty that led to an ideological split and a Civil War more vicious by far than even the bloodiest events of the War of Independence. For when it came to execution without trial, assassination in cold blood, and the persecution of innocent civilians for the transgressions of their relatives, the Irish showed that they had nothing further to learn from the departing Black and Tans and their political masters.

We have chosen to begin with this bloody beginning because despite what conventional wisdom has taught, with the deliberate intention of giving us ideas above our true station, we are still floundering in the political aftermath of the Civil War. Our two biggest political parties have their tap-roots in that split and what it led to, and the third one has scarcely left the side-line seat it chose for itself in 1918.

All other political parties and manifestations, present and deceased, grew out of what is sometimes called "the post Civil War situation" which is only a long-winded Irishism for "the Civil War". The latest manifestation, the Progressive Democrats, by stressing the desirability of getting away from Civil War politics only draws attention to the fact that Desmond O'Malley's attempt to mould Fianna Fáil to a more Fine Gael image ended in failure; which in turn proved that his accidental membership of Fianna Fáil was a mistake to start with. This is depressing, admittedly, but only depressingly accurate.

Another good reason for setting out from this point is that the strongest and most persistent political force in our state, the Catholic Church and its various lay fronts and pressure groups, tightened its grip on the country's windpipe during these crucial years. We have not spent the recent past on the dark side of the moon and are fully aware that conventional wisdom would have us believe that this grip is more illusory than real in this swinging society with fifty per cent of the population under twenty-five years.

We are constantly led to believe that because a large chunk of the population subscribes to no religious principles whatever, the power of the Church is probably less than that of the features pages of the *Irish Independent*. It may well be true that the majority of our citizens lack moral and social principles, and regard religion as a form of fire insurance, but it is very stupid to imagine that this weakens the political power of the Church. In fact it may even strengthen it.

People of deep conviction are much more likely to question and to answer back; time-serving sycophants, which is what the majority of Irish people really are, will jump to the sound of a distant lash like galley-slaves. Recent events have shown that politicians are as much to blame for this situation as any other body in the state. The same events have shown that most of those who preach from editorial pulpits, and who are not slow to describe themselves as moulders of public opinion, are much more out of touch with the harsher realities of Irish life than the parish priest of Attythomaisreevy who is rarely sober after two o'clock in the day.

Another good reason for choosing to set out from the Treaty is the latest agreement — or is it an accord? —

signed by our Taoiseach and the British Prime Minister, at the end of 1985 in Hillsborough. This is the first serious adjustment of the stepping-stones brought home from London in 1921. They were subsequently altered slightly in shape and in name by Eamon de Valera and John A. Costello, but their direction was not changed. The Loyalists have read the signs rightly, and there is little point in anyone in the south lulling them into a sense of false security: this agreement, if adhered to and developed, means nothing less than the end of their world as they and their forefathers knew it. The fact that the majority of citizens of the Republic, who would regard the prospect of a united Ireland with horror, would react to Loyalist apprehension with a hearty, "May the devil mend them", only goes to show that the future of this island is far from being settled.

But the real irony of this latest agreement is that the man who started the process which led to it, C. J. Haughey, found it necessary to condemn it out of hand when Garret FitzGerald signed it.

An even greater irony would emerge for our mystification if subsequent events proved Haughey right. It is a possibility, but it is also time for us to return to our chosen beginning. . . .

Most contemporary historians seem to agree that the Civil War was not inevitable, even after the Treaty was signed. One wonders to what extent more recent events have affected their attitude. While it is true to say that well-intentioned attempts were made to avoid armed confrontation, four very different forces seemed to combine to force the situation over the brink and into conflict.

The British Government was determined to stick firmly to the letter of the Treaty. It frustrated the efforts of Michael Collins, with the help of some of those bitterly opposed to his stand, to bring about even the vaguest form of peaceful co-existence with the opponents of the Treaty. He countered the accusation that the negotiators had exceeded their authority (and betrayed their oath to the

Republic), in signing without having referred the most contentious sections of the Treaty back to the Cabinet in Dublin, by saying that their signatures did not commit the Dáil.

Such talk scared the British. Having found the answer to the Irish problem, they were afraid that the Irish, with the assistance of some of the delegates who had been bullied into signing, would once again change the question. The British Government had the advantage of knowing exactly how far it would allow the new state to assert its limited independence. It had an eye to its Empire and knew that Indian eyes were smiling in the direction of events in Ireland.

Collins was free to assert that he had brought home a set of stepping-stones to freedom, as long as he did not attempt to demonstrate how the first one worked. When the time came the British Government did not have to push the Free State too hard to turn skirmishing into a full-scale war and demolish the Four Courts. At that stage the Republican garrison had provided a reason of its own; apart from the assassination of Sir Henry Wilson for which Collins and not the Four Courts garrison was probably responsible. The kidnapping of General J. J. O'Connell, Deputy Chief of Staff of the Free State Army, led to the shelling of the Four Courts with British guns.

This final footnote to a phase in recent history proved remarkably prickly some thirty-five years later, when the commentary for the Gael-Linn film, *Saoirse?* was being written. Those borrowed guns were almost airbrushed out of history. One could imagine Liam Mellows muttering the Galway proverb, "Bíonn grásta san áit go mbíonn náire" (Grace is found where there is shame).

The non-Republican, non-IRA and non-IRB faction in the struggle for independence, whose figure-head was Arthur Griffith, had no difficulty in swallowing the oath to the Republic, recently imposed on them by those who did not trust them. As far as they were concerned the Treaty was a definite improvement on any previous British offer.

Griffith was much less concerned about the Northern problem than his fellow-delegates.

His ill-advised note to Lloyd George, agreeing to a Boundary Commission as sufficient guarantee that the Northern state had no future, was signed without the knowledge of his fellow-delegates. At that stage he could have admitted an indiscretion, resigned from the delegation and gone home. This would probably have led to a renewal of the war with Britain, which no matter how one looks at these events today, seems the only alternative to Civil War. However, Griffith never believed in the Republic and the delegation decided to hang in together and be responsible for the best negotiated bargain they could bring home. On the Northern issue, the one issue on which they could possibly break off negotiations, they were conned.

The third force was composed of various sections in the community who had a stake in the country and were weary of uncertainty and war. Some of them never wanted a war. Many of them had deserted the sinking ship of the Irish Party without having any clear idea of what Sinn Féin would actually achieve. They were carried away by a sudden wave of national enthusiasm. Now a perfectly safe harbour appeared in front of them.

Far from making any sense politically, an oath to a Republic would strike most of them as being vaguely pagan and not in any way as respectable as an oath to a well-established monarchy.

The Catholic Church, with the exception of a handful of militant curates, was dragged into the national struggle for independence by the canonicals and did not like it one bit. The threat of conscription exposed them to irresistible pressure from their flock who objected to having their skins, and the skins of their offspring, permanently perforated for the freedom of small nations far from home. The Church wanted peace, and as quickly as possible, to enable the bishops to concentrate their efforts on nailing down the new state with their croziers.

Their Protestant counterparts made less noise (they were in training to learn due humility) but they too found the prospect of a Free State, with the protection of the King to boot, infinitely preferable to the nebulous Republic.

The business classes of all denominations, the newspaper proprietors, the professional classes, all wanted peace and the formation of any kind of stable state. Those lower down the social scale saw the prospect of good pensionable jobs in the civil service, the army, the police force, and local government. The British were leaving weren't they? What was good enough for Mick Collins was good enough for them. Very shortly, some of them were going to get the opportunity to shoot other Irishmen to prove that very point.

But the powder-keg required to provide the necessary initial explosion was supplied by the dedicated Republicans who regarded their oath to the Republic as sacred and binding unto death. When all attempts at compromise failed they merely had to provoke the Free State, backed by the British Government and the other forces mentioned above, into making war on them.

Much has been written about the confusion surrounding the Republic that was at the heart of the Civil War. What did it really mean? Did anyone understand clearly, even those most dedicated to its establishment? Lloyd George, at his most unhelpful best, wanted to know if there was a word for it in Irish.

One can only argue through examples. It is clear that de Valera was not a Republican in the sense that Rory O'Connor, Liam Lynch or Liam Mellows were, and that while de Valera would have been much closer to Collins, on this issue, than Collins was to Griffith, de Valera would have wished to tread a different set of stepping-stones: no more than that.

Who could forget the occasion when de Valera, as Taoiseach, came into Dáil Eireann and with the aid of a pile of dictionaries proved that what existed in the twenty-six county reality (and presumably in the thirty-two county myth) corresponded in every detail with every definition of a Republic. Yet, when the Republic of Ireland was declared to exist officially, in 1949, de Valera was not at all pleased. At this stage he probably realised that neither dictionaries nor acts of the Oireachtas were going to "take the gun out of politics", which was the purpose of the Republic of 1949.

Putting it at its simplest, the men in the Four Courts and most of those who supported them, saw themselves as Republicans in the tradition of Wolfe Tone. They wanted the British presence removed from the island of Ireland and physical force was their chosen instrument. In this they followed Tone; a fact which seems to have escaped the leader-writers of the *Irish Times* who have re-created a D'Olier St version of Tone leaving out this important ingredient. Once the British presence was removed, an egalitarian form of government would be established for all Ireland.

A lot of these men distrusted politics and politicians. Compromise was close to treachery in their lexicon. Some of them, as we shall see, had a broader outlook and were beginning to develop a social policy. What they lacked was a clear view of how the Loyalist-Protestant population of the North was to be accommodated in their Republic.

In this they were not alone. If the Northern question was swept aside by a subterfuge in London, it scarcely figured in the long and frequently acrimonious debate in the Dáil. Everyone believed, or seemed to believe, that the new state was irrelevant and could not last. Once the question of British sovereignty and the oath of allegiance to the Crown was resolved the Six Counties were going to fall into the lap of the southern state with the assistance of the British Government. So the TDs devoted their attention to symbols and forms of words and avoided the one issue of substance which could have possibly united the majority of them. Even as matters stood the Treaty was only carried by a majority of seven.

The personal animosities that emerged so quickly and so

clearly during that debate could not possibly have blossomed overnight. The seeds of a confrontation had been sown before the negotiations on the Treaty commenced. It would have been a considerable help had all the parties concerned been clear in their own minds, and particularly in their communications with their colleagues, about what they were setting out to achieve and what the bottom line for breaking off negotiations would have to be.

On the Irish side (apart from the Northern Loyalists who were getting exactly what they wanted) there was great confusion, a sense of having been led astray and divided beyond repair and a deep feeling of doom. Collins had a fairly clear vision of what the future held for him and, by implication, for many of his present and past comrades.

After signing the Treaty he wrote to a friend, John O'Kane, obviously in the depths of despair. "Will anyone be satisfied at the bargain? Will anyone? I tell you this — early this morning I signed my death warrant."

Some historians, apart from those who lay the blame for the Civil War squarely on his shoulders, have given de Valera a leading role in the events leading up to it and in the conduct of the war itself. This may be good politics but scarcely good history. De Valera had very little say in the matter. He had the choice of stepping out of politics completely (something he frequently spoke of doing but never did), or doing what he did: becoming the prestigious figurehead of a movement that had its own momentum, and which only military defeat could stop.

By doing this de Valera ensured that he would become the political leader of a substantial group of dedicated people. Later he would lead them in a new effort to change the shape and the direction of those stepping-stones. But first there had to be a Civil War. . . .

Even before it started Michael Collins caught a glimpse of what the future had in store for the new Northern state. Having been given a sturdy British boot to place on the necks of the Catholic minority inside the state, with a sturdy British foot to keep it from slipping, the assassination squads began to slaughter Catholics while the south argued about symbols.

Collins did his best to get as many guns as possible into the hands of the IRA inside the North, although this clearly broke the terms of the Treaty. His only concern was the protection of the Catholic population. Even his Republican enemies admitted that he asked no questions about the political loyalties of those who were going to use them. He could see that in their situation such loyalties mattered not at all. At this stage he must have almost welcomed the death he seemed to court before the fatal ambush at Béal na Bláth.

After his death the Civil War entered its vicious stage. The Free State government decided that the new state needed a blood-bath and it set out to put down Republicanism with a reign of terror. It was scarcely necessary. The Republicans had little going for them apart from an appetite for martyrdom. There was no military plan. The forces in the country lacked the capability to hold the one strategic position they needed to mount a serious campaign: Limerick City. The forces in Dublin were depending on Joseph Mary Plunkett's original plan for the 1916 Rising and Liam Mellows seemed to favour martyrdom in the ruins of the Four Courts.

They seemed to be unaware that unlike the War of Independence, which was in essence a political war, this one was going to be decided by military might and tactics. Before long the Republicans were back in the hills being hunted by zealous forces with superior equipment who knew the terrain as well as they did themselves. When captured they found that their interrogators were men like Nelligan, who had been recruited and trained by Michael Collins to run to earth and exterminate what was then a common enemy.

Above all else the Civil War exposed a national inclination to savagery, official and unofficial, which still exists. It is clearly nonsense to say, as politicians of all persuasions do, that violence has no place in our tradition. Such statements are merely part of the myth-making process to convince the gullible that all our wars were conducted with the dignity and decorum of the 1916 Rising until the present war in the Northern State began. All wars are dirty, horrible and degrading. They also seem to be an unavoidable part of human activity and are likely to continue to consume lives and energy until such time as man learns to control the baser elements in his nature. Believers will call this fatal flaw, which shows no sign of mending or being mended, Original Sin.

Because of the myth-making process, to which all politicians, some academics, many writers and most of the mass-media in our state contribute, one must take a closer look at some of the more brutal events of the Civil War. Some of them, on both sides, were as tragic as they were brutal and in any half-civilised society would have long since provided the material for Irish-made feature films. After all, a Polish director of genius, Wajda, made *Ashes and Diamonds*, showing the post-war political tensions in Poland, in much more difficult political and economic circumstances.

Artistic considerations apart, such films would have been far better sermons against the futility of violence and the danger of accepting slogans as a substitute for thought than the jaded platitudes of our politicians. Of course they would have also shown that our state was conceived and born in bloodshed and that out of the violence that opposed its foundation grew the party that legitimised the Civil War a decade after it ended.

2

W. T. Cosgrave, the Pope and God's Granny

Even with the benefit of hindsight it is impossible to establish without doubt that civil war was inevitable once the Treaty was signed. Clearly the necessary ingredients were there, although most people would now agree that war was an excessive conclusion to an argument that concentrated on superficialities and avoided the major issue. What is clear is that the will and the means to avoid armed conflict were not equal to the situation that developed. The Treaty itself became the central issue and the Irish went to war about symbols and forms of words that meant different things to different people.

The only political grouping in the emerging state to avoid involvement and to devote its efforts to peace-making, the Labour Party, has hardly prospered as a result of its good intentions and good works. Both the warring factions won something; the Labour Party was the loser.

The conflict lasted only ten months. In that short space of time a level of bitterness was reached which is still not easy to comprehend. British historians have made great play with the statistics: twenty-four Republican prisoners executed by the British in three years to seventy-seven executed by the Free State in less than ten months, most of them without even the semblance of a trial.

In a country with a strong inclination towards different forms of martyrdom, as an end as well as a means to an end, the messianic ferocity and fervour of the betrayed Republicans is easier to understand than the calculated savagery of the new Government. When the fighting started it seems likely that a majority of citizens was in favour of using controlled violence to put an end to the Republicans' military campaign, such as it was.

But some of the methods used by the Government succeeded in turning many of those people against them for the simple reason that they regarded the methods as brutal and excessive. The special emergency powers which allowed military courts to impose the death penalty, and have it carried out, for a wide range of offences, seem draconian even by contemporary South African standards, but variations on such laws became part of the paraphernalia of the new state, under different governments, up to the present day. The Northern state assembled its own unique Special Powers for its own reasons.

A terrible beauty was certainly not born in the early 1920s but terrible precedents were certainly created, in both states.

The purpose of the Free State's special powers was to end the conflict quickly. But they were used in such a way as to raise doubts about part of the motive. The attendant brutality, and particularly the torture of prisoners, owed as much to a desire for revenge, inflamed by these uncomfortable reminders of the recent past, as to a desire to achieve a return to normality.

Whatever the full reasons, and whatever about the Treaty granting the freedom to achieve freedom, it was proved conclusively that under its terms peace between the warring Irish factions was impossible to achieve.

Some members of the new Government showed signs of shame and guilt at finding themselves hunting down old comrades in arms. Others seemed to revel in their power to inflict punishment. Ernest Blythe, one of the Northern nationalists to make his mark in the South at the time, tried to bring institutionalised savagery to its logical conclusion by suggesting that the killing of prisoners in retaliation for the killing of Free State soldiers by Republicans should be carried out secretly, without any official identification of the prisoners concerned, and that their remains should then be buried secretly to avoid unseemly and counter-productive demonstrations by their relatives and friends.

The Government stopped short of accepting this clever plan to rob death of its sting while accentuating it, but extended a form of it to Kerry where the war had reached new heights of viciousness by the Spring of 1923.

"Prisoners who die in military custody in the Kerry command shall be interred by the troops in the area in which death has taken place."

This came after one of the most shocking incidents of the Civil War, which would probably have remained a mystery forever but for an extraordinary accident. Because of it one man lived to tell the gruesome tale of what happened at Ballyseedy Cross.

The events that led to this episode give a picture of what state the war had reached. Republican forces in the Knocknagoshel area of Kerry attached a trigger-mine to a dump and lured a Free State patrol to the spot. According to a statement issued later by the Republicans, the intention was to kill a named lieutenant who, as the statement put it, "had made a hobby of torturing Republican prisoners in Castleisland." The explosion killed the lieutenant, two captains and two private soldiers.

At the time, a group of Republican prisoners was under interrogation in Ballymullen Barracks in Tralee. They were all beaten, some of them subjected to mock-execution, and one received spinal injuries that rendered him unable to walk. In fact his injuries saved his life.

At various stages, after the Knocknagoshel killings, nine prisoners were shown their coffins, having been summarily sentenced to death. However, sentence was not carried out and instead they were herded into a lorry one day before dawn and driven out the Castleisland Road. An officer told them they were going to dismantle a barricade. This they did not believe as one of them had a broken shoulder, another a broken wrist, and all of them were suffering from severe beatings.

The lorry pulled up alongside Ballyseedy Wood, where the prisoners saw a tree-trunk lying across the road. They were taken out and assembled around it with their backs against it. They were bound hand and foot, with rope and electric flex, and then bound tightly together with a heavy rope. They realised from the movements of the soldiers that something was being placed behind them and suspected the worst. They had begun to pray when the landmine went off.

Stephen Fuller was one of four Republicans captured a month earlier in a dug-out. One of his companions on the occasion, John Shanahan, was the prisoner whose injuries saved him from the trip to Ballyseedy. The explosion was followed by shrieks of pain, then there was silence. Stephen Fuller realised he was alive, blown clear of the men on either side of him into a ditch. The soldiers had no way of knowing that a prisoner was missing. All that remained on the spot, and in the trees overhead, can best be left to the imagination.

The soldiers returned to Tralee and came back to Ballyseedy with nine coffins. The official story was that nine Republicans were killed as they prepared an ambush for Free State forces. Stephen Fuller's name was on one of the coffins. But while the soldiers were gone Stephen Fuller crawled away to safety and in time the story of what really happened at Ballyseedy became known. An elaborate memorial now marks the spot.

It was because of the scenes in Tralee later that day, when relatives fought with soldiers and opened some of the coffins, as well as the scenes of grief and anger at the funerals later, that the new regulation was issued to the Kerry command.

Stephen Fuller was elected Fianna Fáil TD for Kerry North, in 1937 and 1938, but lost his seat in 1943. A well-known Kerry footballer, with strong Republican sympathies, took a seat for the first time in the Labour interest. His name was Dan Spring.

At this time the Republican fervour that the Civil War generated in Kerry (nineteen prisoners in all were put to death in the county in the week that the Ballyseedy killings were carried out) had entered a new phase. Fianna Fáil, in the person of the lone survivor of Ballyseedy, was paying the penalty for having imported the British hangman, Pierpoint, to execute Maurice O'Neill from Cahirciveen. He had been involved in a gun battle with detectives in Dublin in which one detective was shot dead.

Serious doubts were raised at the trial as to whether the shot that killed him had been fired by O'Neill at all. But the Military Tribunal that tried him regarded that as a matter of little interest. Time had passed, but times had not changed all that much.

It was the introduction of the special emergency powers that led to the best-known act of retaliation by the Free State Government: the execution of Liam Mellows, Rory O'Connor, Dick Barrett and Joe McKelvey in Mountjoy Jail on 8 December 1922. It was commemorated in verse by Monsignor Pádraig de Brún, one of the few Catholic priests to support the Republican side publicly.

The Republicans declared open season on the TDs who had voted in the special measures and one of them, Seán Hales, died of gunshot wounds received as he was going to attend the Dáil. The Cabinet decided that the Republicans had to be taught a severe lesson and four prominent prisoners were chosen for summary execution. Peadar O'Donnell, who was a prisoner in the jail at the time, wrote a vivid account of the affair in his book, *The Gates Flew Open*.

Even at this early stage the Catholic Church had entered into the fray with threats of excommunication for Republicans. Liam Mellow's attempts to receive the sacraments before his execution, without compromising his political beliefs, are almost as harrowing as his botched execution by a nervous firing-squad.

Most of the blame for this reprisal, and others that followed, (the earlier execution of Erskine Childers was clearly an act of vengeance) was laid at the feet of two members of the cabinet, Ernest Blythe and Dick Mulcahy. Blythe, in his straightforward way, made no attempt to conceal the part he played in strengthening the backbones of some waverers, who seemed to regard the summary execution of prisoners as a form of murder no different to the shooting of Seán Hales.

Mulcahy was more reticent about his role. It was public opinion, fed on rumours, that dubbed him "Dirty Dick" and the cry "Seventy-seven" followed him through all his political life. Although he was leader of Fine Gael when the Coalition Government of 1948 was being formed, Clann na Poblachta refused to have him as Taoiseach and John A. Costello, who only said that the Blueshirts would triumph in Ireland as the Brownshirts succeeded in Germany, was chosen instead.

The choice of the four prisoners was also symbolic, as they were supposed to represent the four provinces. But although Liam Mellows led a small rising in Galway in 1916 he was a native of Wexford. As there was no shortage of genuine Connacht prisoners in Mountjoy at the time, there was always more than a suspicion that Mellows was a marked man for other reasons.

While he was a prisoner in Mountjoy Mellows, at the request of Peadar O'Donnell and others, wrote an outline of what he thought Republican social policy should be when the time came to re-build the movement. In his book, *There Will Be Another Day*, Peadar O'Donnell describes the background to what became known as "Notes from Mountjoy Jail":

In the angry mood of the thronged cells in Mountjoy Jail the prisoners instinctively turned to Mellows as the one among us who must, somehow, be able to explain how the Republican Army could permit itself to be overrun by much weaker military forces and why certain men of courage, hitherto devoted to Independence, should choose to enter on a road of struggle to overthrow the

22

Republic and raise on its ruins a parliament which rested on the penal British Government of Ireland Act 1920.

Mellows jotted down a series of headlines in three different letters which were smuggled out of the prison but which fell into the hands of the Free State authorities. They released them to the press with a covering note drawing attention to the suggested programme for the redistribution of land and the confiscation of the big estates, and anything else that smacked of socialism which, for the sake of convenience and a better smear, became Communism. His attack on the Catholic Hierarchy spoke for itself, "... their exaltation of deceit and hypocrisy, their attempt to turn the noble aspect of Irish struggle and bring it to the level of putrid politics, their admission that religion is something to be preached about from pulpits on Sundays, but never put into practice in the affairs of the Nation, their desertion of Ulster...."

What were these "Notes from Mountjoy" really about? They were really no more than a re-statement of the Democratic Programme of the First Dáil with a little less reverence for the sanctity of private property than that watered-down document displayed. Because of the difficulty the reader may have in finding these brief notes — outside of Mellows' biography and some pamphlets — it is worth giving a key section here.

We should certainly keep Irish Labour for the Republic; it will be possibly the biggest factor on our side. Anything that would prevent Irish Labour becoming imperialist and respectable will help the Republic. As a sidelight on Johnson, O'Brien, O'Shannon and Co. it will interest you to know that when they called on us in the Four Courts last May they (particularly Johnson) remarked that no attempt had been made by the Dáil to put its Democratic Programme into execution. In our efforts now to win back public support to the Republic we are forced to recognise — whether we like it or not — that the commercial interests so-called — money and gombeen men — are on the side of the Treaty, because the Treaty means Imperialism and England. We are back to Tone — and it is just as well — relying on that great body "the men of no property". The "stake in the country" people were never with the Republic. They are not with it now — and they will always be against it — until it wins!

Of course Liam Mellows was neither a Communist nor an advanced Socialist. But he did have a deep contempt for the gombeen class which was about to sink its fangs in the divided country's neck. Mellows represented the Tone-Fenian tradition but did not share the more extreme militants' distrust of politics, disguised as contempt for politicians who would always sell out those who had borne the brunt of the military campaign.

Arthur Griffith, with his dislike for organised labour and his reverence for crowned heads of state, stood at the opposite pole from Mellows. Before 1923 had dawned both men were dead. But the forces that Griffith represented triumphed; what Mellows stood for has been abandoned by a Labour Party content to wait at the gombeen man's table, and not really articulated by a Workers Party that is more of an ideological conspiracy than a national political party.

The fighting ended and the dead were buried. The jails were so full of Republican prisoners that at one stage the Government thought of asking the British for the loan of St Helena to accommodate their surplus Napoleons. Many of those released could find no work and emigrated to the United States to set a fuller cauldron of bitterness simmering on a slow but constant flame.

One unlikely man got a very good job in the new Free State, as well as a new lease of political life. Many people, not all of them Republicans by any means, saw the appointment of Tim Healy as Governor General of the

Irish Free State as some sort of diabolical judgement on what had happened in the country since the turn of the century. For in any competition to name the five most despicable people in Irish public life during that period, Tim Healy would have headed most people's list.

The man who threatened to drive Parnell into the grave or into the lunatic asylum, and having succeeded in the first aim referred to his victim's widow as "that British prostitute", was now the King of England's understudy in Ireland.

> Who was it killed the Chief?
> Said the Sean Bhean Bhocht
> Who was it cried stop thief?
> Said the Sean Bhean Bhocht
> 'Twas Tim Healy's poisoned tongue
> Our chieftain dead that stung
> Better men than him were hung
> Said the Sean Bhean Bhocht.

A relative of Parnell's had horsewhipped Healy publicly after the insult to Kitty O'Shea, but now the new state had more than made up for the weals. A Northern journalist, St John Ervine, described Healy as having, ". . . a sort of purity which became nauseous because it was unaccompanied by any kind of charity. This bitter tongue leapt out of his mouth when he spoke of anyone who had fallen into mortal sin; and when he referred to a woman who had offended against the law, he did so in terms that made even the strong of stomach feel sick."

Once during idle conversation in London, Winston Churchill asked Michael Collins if he had any plans for the Vice-Regal Lodge. Collins, who was depressed at the time, muttered that he might turn it into a cancer hospital. Now it was going to be known as Uncle Tim's Cabin and the King of Ireland — at one remove — would invite W. B. Yeats to come and meet him "in my bee-loud glade".

After the horror and the bloodshed the begrudgers were

feeling the lack of a bitter laugh and saw that the new state was going to provide the makings of more than one. It was reported that one senior British Government Minister was delighted with Healy's appointment. He heard that the new Governor General placed flowers on the grave of Lord Frederick Cavendish every year on the anniversary of his assassination by the Invincibles, not far from the Vice-Regal Lodge. There was no blotting it out. Tim Healy had the cool head and the long step.

Then, according to a highly-unreliable account furnished to Brendan Behan by a drinking companion of one of the security men, President W. T. Cosgrave went to Rome to inform the Pope in person that he had nailed Ireland—the main part of it, at least—down firmly for God. The Pope probably knew this already from his representatives who had seen to the nailing down themselves.

Another security man, who refused to let his charge out of his sight at any time, and who kept his hand on his gun constantly, was told that he could relax in the Vatican. He replied: "I don't trust those hoors with the hatchets", and that he had heard Mary McSwiney had been seen in Paris. It is not today nor yesterday that security took a high priority in this state.

The Pope wanted to know how Mr de Valera was behaving but Cosgrave had other things on his mind.

"Your Holiness, now that I'm here," he said, "Wait a minute till I tell you about St Anne. We had a great devotion to St Anne in our family. We always called her 'God's Granny'. I wonder was it a sin for us?"

The Pope then remembered that he was told to ask about the progress of the Shannon Scheme. But Mr Cosgrave was not having any of that mundane stuff either.

"Your Holiness, wait till I tell you about St Aloysius. We used to pray to a statue of St Aloysius and we could never make out if he was a boy or a girl. It was the long skirts, you see. I don't suppose it was a sin for us, Your Holiness?"

Afterwards, according to this much-travelled tale, the Pope was very angry with his advisors who had not acquainted him with the Irish President's curious pre-occupation with religion. However, he must have been pleased to be told that Irish politics, as well as religion, now came from Rome.

3

"In God's name, pledge yourself to God against drink!"

It would be misleading to speak of the success of the Catholic Church in gaining a position of strength and influence in the new state without some reference to the special position it held under British rule. For many years the British authorities in Ireland had realised that to administer through responsible native institutions, when that was possible, was to govern wisely and effectively. Nowhere was this more evident than in matters concerning the education of Catholics in the national school system.

The clerical managers of national schools were given the responsibility of hiring, firing, paying and otherwise disciplining the national teachers. The teacher could not have a private life which ran counter to his clerical manager's outlook on life. If he became involved in activities likely to meet with his manager's disapproval, particularly in the field of politics, his days in that particular school — and probably most others in the region — were numbered.

The Irish National Teachers Organisation had for many years been disturbed by what amounted to the instant dismissal of members by clerical managers. After much discussion a general meeting of the Bishops in Maynooth in 1894 adopted a resolution which provided that no three months's notice of dismissal could be served on a teacher by a Catholic clerical manager until the manager had informed the bishop of his intention to take such action and had obtained the agreement of the bishop to serve such notice. The teacher would have the right to be heard in his own defence. This resolution was known as the Maynooth Resolution and was designed to protect teachers against their employers, the clerical managers.

Michael O'Shea was principal teacher of Fanore two-teacher school in September 1914. Fanore is situated half way between Doolin and Black Head, on the coast road to Ballyvaughan. It was a remote spot at the time and the manager, Fr Keran, Parish Priest of Lisdoonvarna, found it difficult to get female assistant teachers for the school, which had a teachers' residence nearly.

On more than one occasion Fr Keran spoke to O'Shea about the desirability of teachers in the same school being married and living in the residence. He said it in such a way that O'Shea got the impression that the manager wished him to marry the assistant. This would have caused some difficulty as he was already engaged to a girl who was not a teacher. On 11 September he wrote to Fr Keran asking his permission to be married in Galway.

Three days later Fr Keran called to the school and spoke to O'Shea outside, in a state of some agitation. Had he forgotten his remarks about marriage and had he considered his tenure in Fanore? The teacher considered the suggestion that his tenure should depend on his marriage to be monstrous.

The priest retorted, "Well then we must part," and when the teacher mentioned the Maynooth Resolution to him he replied, "I'll let you see what protection the Maynooth Resolution will give you." He then went into the school, tore a page from the assistant's copybook, wrote a three months' notice on it and threw it at his principal teacher.

It is as well to emphasise, at this stage, that the above account of the day's events, published by Michael O'Shea two years later, was never challenged or denied. The present writer is obliged to the official history of the INTO for most of the facts of the case. The comments and expansions are, of course, his own.

Instead of going immediately to the local branch of the INTO with his strange story, O'Shea wrote to the Bishop of Galway, Dr O'Dea, requesting the protection of the Maynooth Resolution and asking for permission to be married in Galway. Some days later he received a strange reply from the Bishop:

"I am informed that there is no longer a desire for the marriage and that your school has been reported as very discreditable. This is a serious matter for the school and apparently due to a cause which no one can tolerate."

Michael O'Shea replied in writing, informing the Bishop that his marriage was definitely arranged and enclosing copies of his very satisfactory school reports for the Bishop's information.

The Bishop wrote back promising to look into the matter, but weeks passed in silence as O'Shea's three months' notice ran out. By now the teacher had an additional complaint. At this time, and for years afterwards, teachers' salaries were paid quarterly, through the manager to the teacher, after the manager had signed the quarterly returns from the school. It was a form of financial control which was much resented and which was frequently used to remind teachers of their true station in life.

Fr Keran was refusing to pass on the cheque for the September quarter, as well as money spent on repairs to the school and residence by O'Shea and sanctioned by Fr Keran. O'Shea wrote a letter of complaint to the Bishop who avoided the issue in his reply:

"I am sorry for the unpleasantness between you and the parish priest. I would remind you that the important question is whether your discharge of your duties as teacher has been such as to permit of your retention."

Yet another letter was sent to the Bishop about the unpaid salary. At the end of November he replied, "I should be very sorry that you were left unpaid for a day and I am writing to the parish priest accordingly."

It is worth pointing out, at the risk of breaking the chronological order of events, that O'Shea eventually received his salaries for the September and December quarters at the end of May 1915, after a solicitor's letter was sent to Fr Keran.

At the beginning of January, when the dismissal notice had expired, and another teacher appointed in his place, O'Shea received another letter from the Bishop, still ignoring the school reports but introducing a completely new charge against him:

> From enquiries I have made, I am satisfied I ought not to interfere in favour of your retention. I can say in all truth that I regret this extremely for your sake. May I say as your Bishop, and solely from regard for your interest that you can have a splendid future in spite of this set back. As far as I know there is only one thing necessary. In God's name, when you read this, pledge yourself to God against drink for a year and then for life. Our Lord gave up more for you and the reward here and hereafter is surely worth the sacrifice. May God give you the grace to promise and to persevere.

Now O'Shea decided to call on the Bishop in person but, according to his own account, found him vague but unyielding. When O'Shea again demanded the protection of the Maynooth Resolution the Bishop asked if it formed part of the agreement signed by the manager. When told that it did not, he replied, "Then it has no force in law," and said the matter was closed.

The INTO, at local branch and national level, was now involved in the case and a deputation met Dr O'Dea in Ennistymon at the end of January 1915. Michael O'Shea was not present.

The INTO regarded it as a most unsatisfactory meeting. The Bishop informed them that he had never heard of the Maynooth Resolution until O'Shea mentioned it to him — this despite the fact that he was a professor in Maynooth before his appointment as Bishop of Galway. He also refused to state the reasons for O'Shea's dismissal.

When the Executive of the INTO considered the case in February, the General Secretary, Mr Mansfield, wrote to the Bishop asking for another interview and pointing out that there seemed to be no reason for the teacher's dismissal.

It was at this stage that Dr O'Dea gave his first impersonation of the "kind policeman", seeming anxious to settle the dispute. However, there was to be no loss of face and the unproven allegations against O'Shea were repeated. He informed the INTO that there were no grounds for doubt about the reasons for the dismissal. He had verified the facts independently of the parish priest and took the advice of two of his vicars. But neither the teacher, nor the INTO deputation, were told what the facts were or who, apart from the school manager, had advised Dr O'Dea on the matter.

Dr O'Dea did come clean about the Maynooth Resolution. He had looked it up after the Ennistymon meeting, regretted his misconception and promised that if another case arose he would enforce its terms. He suggested that O'Shea take a school "where this unhappy case will not be against him", and that O'Shea should meet him in Lisdoonvarna on 4 March to discuss the matter.

The meeting took place and O'Shea agreed to accept a suitable school away from Fanore. It seemed that although an injustice was done — and O'Shea was still at the loss of six months' salary — at least some restitution was offered in good faith and accepted in that spirit also. But the Bishop had some interesting cards up his sleeve and was in no great hurry to put O'Shea out of his obvious misery.

On May Day 1915, a deputation from the North Clare branch of the INTO met the union Executive at its meeting in Dublin, and briefed it fully on all the circumstances of the Fanore Case, as it was now known. The Executive agreed that the teacher had been very harshly treated and voted him a grant in lieu of salary. Mr

Mansfield wrote to the Bishop and asked him to find another school for O'Shea. The Bishop, once again changing direction, wrote to say that the North Clare deputation had grossly misled the Executive. According to his information, which he still refused to divulge, the facts of the case were common property.

When the North Clare deputation received a copy of this letter they wrote to the Bishop asserting that they could not find a reason for the dismissal. However, now that the Bishop claimed that the facts were common property there could be no justification for withholding them. The Bishop chose to ignore this letter. Events in Fanore were about to cause him that which no Irish bishop could stomach: acute public embarrassment.

The majority of the parents in Fanore stood by the teacher. Out of 80 pupils on the rolls, 50 were sent daily to the teacher's residence for tuition. When the manager evicted him from the residence another house was found, furnished as a residence for O'Shea and his wife with an additional room fitted out as a classroom. The parents promised as much financial assistance as they could afford.

The Bishop reacted furiously. The parents by this action were undermining the case against O'Shea completely. Those who sent their children to O'Shea's house were denounced from the altar in Fanore. When Confirmation time came and the teacher took his pupils to Ballyvaughan, Dr O'Dea ostentatiously refused to confirm them because they were attending a school not sanctioned by him.

And in a final effort to put the fear of God into the courageous people of Fanore, a letter from the Bishop was read to them at Mass threatening to deprive them of the sacraments if they continued to defy their priests and their Bishop.

The case had now assumed scandalous proportions but in August, when all schools were closed for holidays the traditional "friendly priest" arrived on the scene offering to mediate between the North Clare branch and the Bishop. Father Cassidy, Parish Priest of Kilfenora, communicated with the Bishop who immediately smiled his false smile and proffered an olive branch in which some poisoned berries were concealed.

He wished to end the strife. If the opposition school was abandoned immediately and if he got evidence of a change in what had caused the trouble with O'Shea, and if the teachers trusted him, "I shall do all I can to get him a school at least equivalent to Fanore."

On the advice of the branch, O'Shea wrote to the Bishop and accepted his conditions. In return he received, through Fr Cassidy, a pledge against drink he was required to sign. He refused to sign it in its original form, but on the advice of the branch added a sentence protesting against the clear implication that he was addicted to drink.

Before he signed he was told that he could have a choice of two or three schools; after he signed he was offered one, take it or leave it. Far from being "at least equivalent to Fanore" it was a tiny island school, off Ros Muc, with an average attendance of 12 and no residence. Naturally enough, O'Shea refused the offer and on 8 September 1915, had his last communication from Bishop O'Dea, a telegram: "You have had your offer: any other employment whatsoever impossible in these dioceses. I am instructing manager to fill vacancy (Ros Muc) immediately."

O'Shea replied at once, stating that the telegram not only ended negotiations but also ended, as far as he was concerned, the terms of the agreement. All further efforts to deal with Dr O'Dea ended in failure; even the "friendly priest" withdrew from the unequal struggle.

The INTO stood by Michael O'Shea financially as he tried to earn a living in Fanore. This too was an unequal struggle.

The refusal to confirm his pupils, as well as the threatened withdrawal of the sacraments, had the desired effect on the attendance at his school. Some brave parents stood by him to the end but it was a conflict lay people could not win. When the Gaelic League offered him a job as a teacher of Irish under their auspices he decided to accept. The INTO paid him a lump sum of £500 in full discharge of any further claim on the organisation.

Shortly after the establishment of the Free State a Model School was established in Cork City and Michael O'Shea was appointed an assistant teacher. He was held in the same high esteem there as he was in Fanore, even after his match-making manager blighted his life. The INTO made good the reduction of his pension caused by the loss of service before his appointment in Cork. This continued up to the time of his death.

The story requires few footnotes but certain aspects of it call for comment.

First, there is the total absence of any civilian presence, apart from his union, to which Michael O'Shea could turn for protection. The Board of Education is as conspicuous by its absence as Fr Keran became after instigating the trouble. Fr Keran was clearly an incompetent, hysterical but very vindictive man. There was no better way of putting a noose around a young married man's neck than to deprive him of the money he had earned. Why the state allowed such a situation to exist can only be explained by saying that it suited the state to leave such power in clerical hands.

The Bishop's efforts to find a reason for O'Shea's dismissal, other than the Parish Priest's mental aberration, are full of hidden significances. It had to be the drink: a good man's weakness but the ruination of many a promising rebellion, not to mention a promising career. The drink would do nicely but not to make too much of a public issue of it!

No wonder his reaction to the parents who sent their children to the alternative school, even after he had publicly humiliated them in Ballyvaughan Church, was so savage. To threaten them with the ultimate ecclesiastical sanction seems, in the circumstances, excessive. But he was enraged, for the demonstration of support gave the lie to his mean and furtive innuendoes concerning O'Shea's fondness for drink.

He realised that only a competent and highly-regarded teacher could claim such allegiance in such grim circumstances, taking into account the place religion had in their lives and the thin line that separated superstitious fear from genuine belief in rural communities at the time, when the Bishop threatened from the altar.

Giving Bishop O'Dea the benefit of the doubt, and accepting for a moment that he believed that O'Shea had a problem with drink, consider the callous cynicism of an offer of a job on an island in an area where poitín was as plentiful as tea! When one considers that Bishop O'Dea had more than a nodding acquaintance with "demon rum" it gives the whole episode a touch of psychotic gloom.

This incident will go some way towards explaining the militant nature of the INTO which, during the most recent teachers' dispute, was seen as making the running for the other unions. Whether it did or not matters little. The fact is that the INTO is tough because of its history, and the fact that it had to take on Church and State, frequently on ground not of its own choosing.

The teachers' strike of 1946 concerned rates of pay and its aftermath contributed to the sudden flowering of Clann na Poblachta within two years. That happening belongs in a later chapter. What concerns us here is the role of the Catholic Church in the primary school system and it would be pleasing to report that lay teachers were treated better in a native state than they were in 1914.

The last great confrontation between the INTO and a bishop occurred in Ballina in 1956, when the seven teachers in the local primary school returned from their holidays to find that the school had been handed over to the control of the Marist Brothers, The INTO objected on two grounds: that the change was made furtively and without consultation, and that a large lay-controlled school was handed over to an Order, thereby reducing the promotional prospects of the staff. The INTO had been worried for some time by the tendency to hand the larger schools over to religious orders. In 1943 they made a formal complaint to the hierarchy and were informed that, as a rule, the bishops did not favour such transfers.

The Ballina affair seemed to the INTO to be a step backwards to the bad old days and it decided that an immediate strike was the only answer. But after an appeal by the Archbishop of Dublin, Dr McQuaid, the INTO suspended the strike and agreed to appeal to Rome. The organisation felt it owed Dr McQuaid a favour since the Dublin teachers' strike of 1946. He had tried to mediate in that bitter dispute until Mr de Valera gave him a belt across the knuckles with his own crozier and told him to mind his own business.

The 1946 strike was about teachers' pay and the bishops felt free to give the INTO moral support on an issue that did not diminish their own authority and was not a conflict between Church and State. But in Dr McQuaid the teachers felt they had a genuine friend, for when they had to return to work unconditionally he did his best to ease their humiliation with a statement praising their dedication to their vocation.

The INTO felt that Dr McQuaid had a genuine interest in their latest grievance also and were pleased when Rome requested him to mediate. The Archbishop drafted an agreement which satisfied the INTO but which was thrown back at Dr McQuaid by the Bishop of Killala, Dr O'Boyle.

For the benefit of those not familiar with the internal command-structure of the Catholic Church in Ireland it must be pointed out that just as Dr O'Dea had to respect the lunatic decision of the Parish Priest of Lisdoonvarna, and tried to put a slightly saner gloss on it, the Archbishop of Dublin had to respect the authority and the autonomy of the Bishop of Killala. And while Dr O'Dea tended to be occasionally tired, it must be said that Dr O'Boyle was occasionally very emotional.

The INTO then called its threatened strike which dragged on until 1962 when Dr Patrick Hillery, then Minister for Education, worked out a peace formula. Under this agreement the religious headmaster remained in the school and the Bishop of Killala agreed to pay an additional salary to the lay staff member who would have been in line for the principalship.

It could hardly be called a victory for the INTO but it is a fact that no other lay-controlled school was subsequently handed over to a religious order. The real irony of the affair is that it happened just before the teaching orders began to run out of recruits.

At present the tendency is for schools previously controlled by religious orders to be handed over to lay control. This is entirely due to circumstances rather than any change of heart on the part of those who believe that national teachers are the equivalent of the skippers of small coasters, that the big ships sail better under religious control with the odd lay bosun and lay deckhands. Well, they had their day.

The Ballina affair provided an interesting glimpse of how the Church can marshall a section of the laity to provide evidence that the Church is merely responding to popular pressure. No sooner had the school dispute started than an organisation calling itself the Ballina Catholic Parents Association began to issue statements welcoming the Marist Order to the school and implying that not only education but discipline as well would improve with their coming.

This implication played the same role as the piece of paper Michael O'Shea was asked to sign by the Bishop of Galway. But here all similarity with the Fanore case ends. The majority of the Fanore parents stood by the teacher. Those who, for various reasons, did not, had the grace and dignity not to band together in a corps of sanctimonious lick-spittles. Not everything changed for the better in a free Ireland.

4

"A long slow swim
through a sewage bed"

If Tim Healy came to symbolise the tawdriness of the Free State the Censorship of Publications Act 1929, and the Board of Censors it established, became the trademark of its arid philistinism. This was strange because censorship seemed to affect very few people. It caused little hardship and seemed to be of interest only to visiting journalists in search of a beam in Erin's smiling eye, and to that most peevish of minority groups, the writers and intellectuals. And in fact there were some writers who agreed with censorship as it increased the demand for their own unctuous dribblings.

Intellectuals were held in particular contempt. As Seán O'Faoláin pointed out, the worst bomb which could be hurled at one for many years after independence was not the one with "Communist", or even "Republican" chalked on it, but the one which was inscribed, "Yah, Intellectual!" Of course intellectuals had no morals, no strong religious beliefs, no party politics and very little regard for authority; and most of them wrote as well. In fact the term "intellectual" never fully recovered from the first forty years of the freedom to achieve freedom. It still has to be used with a degree of caution; unless, of course, one is applying unction to a political teetotum like Garret FitzGerald.

The initial legislation was not directed at Irish writers, although the trawl it constructed managed to capture them also. The legislation was intended to keep the Irish people pure in mind and tranquil in the most sensitive areas of their anatomy. In short, it was all about Ireland's great preoccupation: the illicit "dart of the other thing", or sex as it is known in the civilised world.

It derived from a report by a Committee on Evil Literature, published in 1927, which found the country awash in pornography and in danger of being scuppered. The Act was passed in 1929 and the Censorship Board founded the following year. The Act provided for a Board of five persons and had the power to prohibit the sale and distribution of any book or periodical it considered "in its general tendency indecent or obscene". It also prohibited the publishing, selling and distribution of literature advocating birth-control.

The first Board consisted of three Catholic laymen, one Protestant clergyman and one Catholic priest. They were equipped with Irish-manufactured filth-detectors and in case of an unforeseen accident the priest was appointed chairman. Although the Protestant Churches were generally in favour of allowing people to choose their own reading material freely, there was always a Protestant presence on the Board to give it a broader look. But as the purpose of the exercise was to control "you-know-what" it would have been difficult for them to object to censorship without giving the impression that they were in favour of indiscriminate and constant fornication — which a lot of Catholics thought they stood for anyway, despite the fact that the southern Protestants were bidding fair to unbreed themselves out of existence.

But Irish writers soon found out that they were the principal victims. When a book by an Irish writer was banned he immediately became a "banned writer" and books and bookshops anticipated public reaction to this new-found pornographer in their midst by keeping all his works off their shelves. There was a myth spread that being banned in Ireland helped to sell a writer's work abroad: that it was an advertisement constantly desired by writers. When the number of books banned ran into thousands, to claim that one was banned in Ireland was rather like boasting that one had actually been offered sex in a brothel.

The hunt for filth and smut was on and there was no shortage of bloodhounds. Vigilance committees scoured libraries and the country's handful of bookshops, underlining passages that seemed to contravene the sacred Act. Customs officials ransacked parcels and purloined likely volumes. Rumour had it that they tried out the dirty bits on their wives in bed before forwarding the books to the Board.

Gradually the country began to look deservedly ridiculous. It began to dawn on people of even limited intelligence that we could no longer blame a foreign power for the lunatic acts being carried out without any official sense of shame. Indeed, the legislators, the vigilance committees and the overworked censors burrowed away like moles in the comforting gloom.

It has been asserted by scholars that no direct connection between the Catholic bishops and the agitation which led to and sustained the Censorship of Publications Act can be established. That may well be the case, although some bishops bleated loudly when the Act was slightly modified.

Since the Knights of Columbanus were founded in 1922 there was no shortage of pressure-groups seeking more and more Government legislation to sustain and to bolster Catholic teaching and to increase the repressed nature of Irish life. A lunatic-fringe Catholic press existed and was encouraged to the extent of being sold in churches and commended from pulpits. These publications were capable of reading filthy double-meanings into the words of "The Bould Thady Quill".

But in fairness — although fairness is not a major obsession in these ruminations — as we pointed out in the case of the Ballina Catholic Parents Association, it is difficult to establish beyond doubt in these matters who is actually the Wizard of Oz and who is the baldy little man with the microphone and the mask pretending to be the

Wizard. One of the fascinating things about this blessed isle of ours is that you cannot even be sure that the man who is charged with murder is actually the man who committed the murder, if it was a murder at all and not an elaborate form of suicide.

In the case of the agitation to rid Ireland of literature, while pretending to fight filth, it is well-nigh impossible to establish whether the laity were doing the bishops' work for them, or whether they were being prodded by invisible ecclesiastical goads.

A personal theory, for all it is worth, is that it was a genuine display of repressed sexuality by people masquerading as religious maniacs, wallowing in the pleasure of being able to legally deprive people of one of civilisation's greatest pleasures: reading widely. One can have pity for people who were suffering from psychological problems they did not understand. It is difficult to extend that act of charity to those who encouraged them and preyed on their disordered minds. One can feel nothing but contempt for the politicians who were willingly led by their noses into this particular blind alley. A quarter of a century was to pass before they began to back out of it in a manoeuvre which deserves the accolade, "The first of the Irish solutions to particularly Irish problems". We shall come to it shortly.

But it took a simple book about a simple couple in West Cork to expose the absurdity of Irish censorship, as well as the infantilism of almost the entire Irish Senate. It would undoubtedly have done the same service for the Dáil had that assembly contained even two members with the courage to propose and second the motion which Sir John Keane, a Protestant landlord from Waterford, put to Seanad Eireann when *The Tailor and Ansty* was banned, shortly after its publication in 1942.

It was written by Eric Cross, an Englishman, who had made friends with the Tailor of Gougane Barra and his wife Ansty, which was short for Anastasia. It was a chronicle of their stories and banter, their observations on life and their conversations and relationships with neighbours and friends. The Tailor was a very well-known person and a noted storyteller in Irish. He had a wide circle of friends, including the banned writer Frank O'Connor, who was among the first to protest publicly at the banning.

Letters were written to the *Irish Times* and Senator Sir John Keane put down a motion that the Censorship Board, "had ceased to retain public confidence, and that steps should be taken by the Minister for Justice to reconstitute the Board".

In an introduction to a later edition of the book Frank O'Connor has likened the reading of the report of the Seanad debate to "a long, slow swim through a sewage bed". He also wrote that he felt he would strain his readers' credulity too much if he quoted from some of the many speeches. That introduction was written in 1964 and in truth, much of what was said was incredible even by 1943 standards of obscurantism. But in view of more recent happenings in our native land, perhaps this version of the fable of the Emperor's New Clothes will not go unappreciated in illiberal circles, at least.

The four-day pantomime started when Sir John Keane insisted on reading those passages from the book which were commonly presumed to have led to its banning. Senator Magennis, who was Professor of Metaphysics at UCD and a member of the Censorship Board, almost lost what little reason God granted him at the thought that these obscenities would appear in the record of the debate and be available to the general public "for a few pence".

Professor Magennis came from Belfast and it was said of him, most unkindly, that he typified the Northern Nationalists who came south at this time who by their every utterance put the desire for Irish unity back a decade in time. What is true is that when the Government chose him as their representative on the Board of the Abbey Theatre, Yeats said he would close the theatre rather than have such a person on its board. To soften this blow to his considerable ego he was nominated to the Senate by

Eamon de Valera and given all the newly-published books in the English-speaking world to play with in his spare time. Mr de Valera, like Mr Cosgrave, regarded literary censorship as part of our freedom to achieve fuller freedom.

The Senate agreed readily to Professor Magennis' suggestion and voted to censor their own record. The debate then started. It is interesting to trace quotations, as some of them can be identified from the report despite the sanitary precautions.

One concerned the Tailor's first visit to the "talking" pictures in Macroom cinema and his comments on what he saw. Adopting the mind of a sex-obsessed censor one can only find one reference of the type likely to earn the label "indecent or obscene" in Ireland at the time. It is most enlightening.

The Tailor found most of the women in the feature film far too thin. A fat lady then appeared and although he found her more appealing she was not entirely to his liking either.

A devil of a great pounder of a woman. She'd make a handy door for a car-house. She'd stifle you in bed. People think that fat women are warm. I tell you they are not. They make a damn great tunnel in the bed, and a man may as well be sleeping in a gully.

When Sir John Keane finished, his isolated position in the House was made clear when his seconder, The McGillycuddy of the Reeks, stood up and said that although he had seconded the motion he did not entirely care for the form in which it was presented. Then the troglodytes entered the fray.

A Senator Goulding thought the book not alone silly and indecent but hopelessly tiresome. He thought it an utter travesty of the Irish countryside and its people. Professor Johnson declared that he was against censorship but admitted to being filled with disgust by the quotations read by Sir John Keane. Professor Liam O'Buachalla said (in

Irish) that the country needed more censorship and (in English) that the general feeling of the house was that the sooner the debate was ended the better. Nevertheless, an awful lot of Senators insisted on speaking at length.

A Senator Kehoe said that ninety per cent of the people did not know the Censorship Board existed, and that only two per cent of the remaining ten per cent had any animus against it. He had read all the authors, as he put it, "from Rabelais down", but a "finer collection of smut" than *The Tailor and Ansty* he had never read. A Senator FitzGerald found the passages read out not alone outrageously immoral but inconceivably boring. He instanced the constant repetition of a phrase about a bull and a cow.

This was a reference to Ansty's surprise when a woman came up to her on the road and asked her if the animal she was minding was a bull or a cow. Ansty was astounded because she had noticed a marriage ring on the woman's finger.

Pádraig O Máille revealed an interesting view of Irish writers. He admired literature when it was literature. The trouble with "second or third rate scribblers" was that to get people to read their books they had to "have a slap at religion or public decency". That was a noted fact about some of our writers who "go across to feed the English public".

At this stage the Minister for Justice, Gerry Boland, intervened to say that it was quite clear from the extracts read in the House that the book deserved to be banned. He congratulated the Board and referred particularly to the banning of *A Land of Spices* by Kate O'Brien.

There had been a lot of comment about the fact that this book was banned on the strength of one passage referring to an embrace between two males. He agreed with the banning because the central theme was "the class of crime" referred to in that passage.

Before dealing with Professor Magennis's contribution one must refer briefly to one of his disciples, Senator Helena Concannon, a writer of lives of the saints. There was no man in Ireland to whom so much was owed, she said. "Gifted with a mighty intellect and a great store of knowledge he could, if personal ambition had been his guiding star, have stayed in his study and written one of the great philosophical works that would have made his name shine forever." She likened the reading of *The Tailor and Ansty* to a torture out of Dante's Inferno.

One is reminded of a review written by this good lady for the *Irish Independent*, in the days when it was the voice of God in Ireland before the advent of the Baron of Flatulence turned it into the voice of Mammon. She concluded a review of a book by a French right-wing Catholic writer with the sentence: "This work is an outstanding contribution to French letters" — an event that almost lost his job for a sub-editor whose mind was far too pure for his own good.

Professor Magennis then rose and stated that the book under discussion was "low and blasphemous". Then he went on to give his metaphysical opinion of Irish writers.

> These men have no ability to write anything but short stories. I grant that some of these men have written fine short stories, but they are not able for the sustained work of a novel and, to make what should be a short story into the voluminous character of a novel to suit the English publishers' demand, they pad it out with sex and smut.

How did this unwholesome trade affect this country? According to the Professor the lending libraries were getting at the public in more ways than one.

> A book that has had its life as a library book in England run to its close starts a new career in Ireland. The entrepreneur in England gets together the books I have indicated and he sends a batch of them here and there to the little country towns of Ireland. They are stocked there in the shops that sell cigarettes, sweets and newspapers and the people of the locality come and borrow them. The shopkeeper is not allowed any choice. He

must take or leave the batch that comes to him, some of them in a most unwholesome condition so far as regards the public health because they have been read by people in sick beds, they may have been read in atmospheres that were rich in bacteria and bacilli, but over they come to this country — it does not matter about us the outlanders — and they are here started on their career of passing on depravity.

Having given a new depth of meaning to the term "dirty books", the Professor casually outlined the world-wide conspiracy that was behind this campaign to deprave.

There is a campaign going on in England to undermine Christianity. It is financed by American money. The society that is the main agent in the endeavour to put in paganism instead of the Christian creed and practice includes Professor Joad and George Bernard Shaw.

When the Professor ended, The McGillycuddy of the Reeks rose to make it clear that he only seconded the motion because Sir John Keane was not sure he could find anyone else to do it and although the motion was contentious it was as well to have a discussion. He wanted to make it quite clear that he had the greatest sympathy with the Board of Censors.

It is a beastly, unpaid, voluntary job and is one which they carry out, to my mind, to the best of their abilities, according to the lights which God has given them, and as a result of it they get more kicks than half-pence.

Then, having freed his collection of clichés, this sorry remnant of the old gentry gave his real views on censorship. They were at least original. The observations of a much-travelled man-mountain.

I think that censorship is definitely necessary. Those who do not think so have only to look to Buenos Aires, in one direction, and Port Said, in another, where there is no censorship. The result in both places is that practically everybody is inoculated with depravity throughout their bodies. I feel that we do not want that, so that censorship must definitely continue. But no censorship will turn what I call a Dirty Dick into a clean one. He will find something obscene and depraving in almost every sentence that he reads, but these Dirty Dicks are few and far between.

When the vote was taken, after a long discussion on whether or not country people talked like the Tailor and his wife, or whether such talk could ever take place when women were present, or whether, as Senator Foran contended, one only met Tailors and Anstys in lunatic asylums, the MacGillycuddy of the Reeks had obviously fled to the ancestral peaks for only Senator Joseph Johnson of Trinity College voted with Sir John Keane. Thirty-four members of our own gentry voted against them.

Three years after this debate an Appeal Board was set up. It had very little effect. Most publishers were reluctant to get involved in a process which would have little influence on sales, even if the appeal was successful. The Board itself continued to ban like blue blazes and between 1950 and 1955 it has been estimated that it hit an average of two books a day.

For the benefit of younger readers it is possibly necessary to point out that almost all Irish writers of note got at least one belt from the Board.

James Joyce (for *Stephen Hero* but not for *Ulysses* which was published before the Act but which was not available in shops or libraries anyway), Seán O'Casey, George Moore, Samuel Beckett, George Bernard Shaw (it was said the *The Black Girl in Search of God* was banned because the Black Girl had no clothes on), Frank O'Connor, Seán O'Faoláin, Liam O'Flaherty, Benedict Kiely, Austin Clarke, John McGahern, Edna O'Brien, Kate O'Brien, Oliver St John Gogarty and Brendan Behan (for *Borstal*

Boy) were among the better known banned

Considerations of space prevent us from g
than a handful of the best-known writers from
living and dead, who had their works stigmatise
Board. There was Freud, de Maupassant, Balzac,
Sartre, Zola, Faulkner, Hemingway, Dreiser, Sa   ger
(for *The Catcher in the Rye*, for God's sakes!), Saroyan,
Maugham, Gide, Gorky, Greene, Durrell, Fitzgerald,
Steinbeck, Dos Passos, Mailer, Capote, Orwell, Moravia
and many, many more, lumped in with the authors of such
classics as *The Shameless Nude*, *Hot Dames on Cold Slabs*, and
Me and My Hot Rod.

The Irish Association of Civil Liberties, which was
established in 1948 to espouse respectable liberal causes,
petitioned the Minister for Justice in 1956 to change the
law on the censorship of publications. James Everett of
Labour was the responsible Minister in the second Inter-
Party Government and being a wise Wicklowman he left
the law alone but appointed two mildly liberal men to the
Board, first marking their cards carefully. Their very
presence infuriated the three others so much that they
resigned rather than see their banning averages fall. They
were replaced by the next Minister for Justice, Oscar
Traynor of Fianna Fáil, who appointed three fairly liberal
substitutes. The result was that the banning average fell to
a little over a book a day.

No legislative changes were made and the Act remained
in force. James Everett could scarcely be called progressive
or excessively intellectual. When Minister for Posts and
Telegraphs in the first Inter-Party Government, he started
the Battle of Baltinglass by appointing one of his supporters
as postmaster in place of a woman whose family had run
the post office for years. He also spoke strongly against
paying large sums of money to "mouth-organ players from
Communist countries" to play in the Radio Eireann
Symphony Orchestra and remarked, more than once, that
his yard-stick for programmes was the man lying on his
settle-bed in Wicklow after his hard day's work. Clearly,

49

...ish solutions to Irish problems were his forte and he deserves his little niche in Irish literary history.

So does Brian Lenihan, who was the next Minister for Justice to give an extra dimension to the Irish solution in 1967.

He introduced a Bill which provided for the removal of the ban on books after twenty years, unless the ban was reimposed. In fact when he saw how few problems he was having in the Dáil he reduced the term to twelve years. This released thousands of books and censorship of serious literature was virtually abolished while retaining the basic legislation intact.

This example of sustained political chicanery was ignored by almost everyone apart from a few cute hoors in Fianna Fáil. Truly Liberal crusaders now insisted on charging windmills head-on instead of creeping in through an unlatched window and turning the sails out of the wind-stream. There was no need for these elaborate Irish subterfuges any more, thank God. The economic boom and the permissive society had changed everything. We even had our own gentry, all dolled up in their nice mohair suits.

Because of these convictions few people paid much attention to two exchanges in Dáil Eireann towards the end of 1967, between the Minister for Education, Donogh O'Malley, and Deputy Oliver J. Flanagan, concerning faith, morals, sexual suggestiveness and bad language; or if they did they thought it-was merely a bit of gas.

It began when Deputy Flanagan told the Minister that parents had complained to him about a textbook, *An Anthology of Short Stories*, used by the Department of Education for Inter-Cert English, and which contained several objectionable words and phrases. Deptuy Flanagan wanted to know what the Minister was going to do about it. During a brief barney, which annoyed Deputy Flanagan, the Minister said he was very happy with the anthology and pointed out that the Committee who recommended it was composed of eminent civil servants and educationalists, including Fr Veale, SJ of Gonzaga

College and Mother Enda of the Dominican Convent, Eccles Street.

All this left Deputy Flanagan unsatisfied and he raised the matter again. This time he came armed with examples. For instance, the following passages from *Guests of the Nation*.

> The capitalists pay the priests to tell us about the next world so that you won't notice what the bastards are up to in this.

> Just as a man makes a home of a bleeding place, some bastard at headquarters thinks you're too cushy and shunts you off.

> Give him his first. I don't mind. Poor bastard, we don't know what is happening to him now,

Also the expressions, "Ah, for Christ's sake", "Poor bugger" and "Then, by God ..." were considered offensive.

Then Deputy Flanagan read two paragraphs from another short story in the anthology which he found "most suggestive".

> She sat up. Stephen was a hot lump of sleep, lazy thing. The Dark Walk would be full of little scraps of moon. She leaped up and looked out the window, and somehow it was not so lightsome now that she saw the dim mountains far away and the black firs against the breathing land and heard a dog say *bark-bark*. Quietly she lifted an ewer of water and climbed out the window and scuttled along the cool but cruel gravel down the maw of the tunnel.

> Her pajamas were very short so that when she splashed water, it wet her ankles. She peered into the tunnel. Something alive rustled inside there. She raced in, and up and down she raced, and flurried, and cried aloud, "Oh, gosh, I can't fit it" and then at last she did. Kneeling down in the damp she put her hand into the

slimy hole. When the body lashed, they were both mad with fright. But she gripped him and shoved him into the ewer and raced, with her teeth ground, out to the other end of the tunnel and down the steep path to the river's edge.

After lambasting the stories he quoted from, and the anthology in general, he asked the Minister to see to it that no suggestive material or vulgar language appeared in future anthologies. The Minister wanted to know if Deputy Flanagan had read the whole of the story he had quoted from and when the Deputy replied, "From cover to cover", the Minister let fly.

> *O'Malley:* The saying: *Honi soit qui mal y pense* was never so appropriate as it is tonight. Does the Deputy, if he has read the story, realise that it is his own vivid and excitable imagination. . . .
> *Flanagan:* No. Parents have written to me.
> *O'Malley:* I would also point out to the Deputy that if he had read the story he would see this young girl is going into the tunnel to catch a trout and not to catch anything else. If these ideas which the Deputy is putting in Irish minds, which no doubt, as on the last occasion, will be widely published in tomorrow's papers, are all he can find in O'Faoláin's "The Trout", which has been described also as the finest story of O'Faoláin, then I can only say, "God help us", and it is a very lucky thing that O'Faoláin and O'Connor cannot combine to write a story on the proceedings here tonight and on the last day. I know that Deputy Flanagan possibly has ambitions in another sphere and that perhaps he hopes one day to be leader of the Knights. [Interruptions].If that is so, I agree that Deputy Flanagan is quite entitled to aspire to such a great office, though anyone using the Catholic Church for his own material or other advancement makes me vomit. I think Our Divine Lord will have certain ideas Himself on these things, because if

there was one thing about Our Divine Lord, it was that he could not tolerate hypocrisy in any form.

Then the Minister proceeded to deal with the objections to some of the expressions quoted from the anthology. He pointed out that some of these words, when preceded by the word "poor", expressed sympathy. Then this exchange took place:

> *O'Malley:* I think the Deputy will agree with that. In the south of Ireland, if one said: 'John fell down a cliff and the poor hoor was killed" —
>
> *Flanagan:* If he is a poor bastard or a poor hoor, he is still a bastard or a hoor.
>
> *O'Malley:* If Deputy Flanagan were down in the south of Ireland at a bye-election, pulled up at the side of the road and was told "John fell down a cliff and the poor hoor was killed" —
>
> *Flanagan:* I would say: "Lord have mercy on him".
>
> *O'Malley:* The Deputy would say rightly: "The Lord have mercy on him". He would not start slagging him for using that type of language. He would say: "The poor hoor, Lord have mercy on him".
>
> *Flanagan:* I would not; I would leave out "poor hoor". I do not care for that type of language.

The pleasantries ended with the Minister again defending the short story described by the Deputy as "suggestive". He concluded with another reference to Deputy Flanagan's state of mind:

"If the mentality of Deputy Flanagan is like that of the unfortunate girl who went into the tunnel to catch a trout, and not to catch anything else, the Lord have mercy on us all."

And all anyone could possibly say to that, even at this stage, is: Amen.

5

"I solemnly swear that this oath is not an oath"

Even as the jails and internment camps bulged with Republican prisoners, the Sinn Féin party suffered a split and the third of a series of sea changes. It was a far cry from 1905 when Arthur Griffith founded a political movement with that name. Rarely, if ever, has the title of a political party served so many different purposes and survived, in various guises, for over eighty years.

The segment of Sinn Féin that accepted the Treaty met in January 1923, and formed Cumann na nGael, which became Fine Gael ten years later. Six months later a meeting in the Mansion House, attended by only 150 people, decided to reorganise Sinn Féin.

At first de Valera was undecided on the matter of fighting the general election but at length, encouraged by public support and promises of money from America, he suggested putting one candidate forward in each constituency. It was also agreed that if Sinn Féin won a majority of seats it would govern the country as in 1919, refusing to cooperate with Britain until Ireland was granted her sovereignty and unity. If the party did not win that majority it would not enter the Free State Dáil but meet apart in a kind of extension of the Second Dáil.

It was clear that Republicans were having difficulty in relating to reality, but that was not their only problem. When the party leader, de Valera, came out of hiding to speak at an election meeting in Ennis he was arrested and spent the next eleven months in jail. Many Republican deputies and candidates were among the 12,000 interned, as well as most of their best organisers. According to Sinn Féin as many as sixty-four of their eighty-five candidates were, for one reason or another, unable to speak to their constituents.

All these circumstances led the Irish and British press to predict that Sinn Féin would win between thirteen and twenty-five seats. But when the votes were counted Sinn Féin had managed to hold forty-four seats out of the total of 153. This came as an unwelcome surprise to the Government. It seemed that they were so unpopular with a section of the electorate that it was willing to vote for people who had no intention of taking their seats. But it was a great boost for Republican morale. Their stand still had support, at home and abroad. The great hunger strike of October and November 1923, in which thousands took part and which lasted forty days (and which claimed the lives of two prisoners) did much to dispel apathy and renew hatred for the Free State.

But the growth of Sinn Féin did not last. By 1924 it had ceased and in 1925 there began a steady decline in funds and membership. Eamon de Valera, Seán Lemass and others saw the policy of abstentionism as the principal reason for this decline and de Valera started a movement to try to wheel the organisation towards a strategy which would get rid of the detested oath.

In May 1925, the Standing Committee of Sinn Féin adopted the resolution which would later cause another schism and lead to the foundation of Fianna Fáil: "That the President may act on the assumption that the question of Republicans entering the Free State 'Parliament' if the oath were removed, is an open question, to be decided on its merits when the question arises as a practical issue".

A section of the IRA had already become disillusioned with this third Sinn Féin party and took a crucial decision. At the first post-Civil War convention of the IRA it was decided — against the wishes of men like Frank Aiken —

that the Army should withdraw allegiance from the Republican "government" and that henceforth the supreme military authority should be the seven-man Army Council, elected by the twelve-man Executive. The Army Council would select the Chief-of-Staff.

There were several reasons for this split. Peadar O'Donnell, for instance, felt that the IRA could play a greater part in Irish life if freed from the "political theorists" of the Second Dáil. Most of those who agreed with him were unhappy with political control, such as it was. The IRA only gave allegiance to the Republican "government" when the Civil War began to go against it, despite its five to one superiority in manpower. It wanted back to the pure Republican source of 1916. Like the Fenians, they felt that political and social issues were distractions from the central military struggle. Politicians were concerned with taboo subjects such as "compromise on principles".

The IRA also anticipated a split on the issue of Dáil participation and wanted the Army clear of it in advance. Its late chief-of-staff, Frank Aiken, admitted to the November Convention that matters related to it were under discussion. After the total and ignominious collapse of the Boundary Commission the troubles of the Cosgrave government increased and the pressure on de Valera for an end of abstentionism became intense. He made one last attempt to carry Sinn Féin with him, but it was doomed to failure. Almost half of Sinn Féin decided to remain pure and undefiled and continue its allegiance to the Second Dáil.

This is as good a place as any to set right some basic misconceptions about Sinn Féin and the IRA. Anyone who ever attended a Sinn Féin Ard-Fheis knows that when a representative from the Army Council attends to read his message he is *telling* Sinn Féin what it is meant to support for the next year. Sinn Féin's main purpose is to muster support for the IRA. Its involvement in any form of politics is secondary and this involvement will be closely and cautiously observed by the Army Council. This will become clearer if and when the present form of Sinn Féin decides to have yet another look at the policy of abstention. These matters will probably come to a head in the North, from which Sinn Féin is now run. Sinn Féin members in the South have no choice but to follow the new leaders or get out of the movement as Seán Mac Stiofáin had to do.

To understand all this is to understand, partly at least, why internal disputes in the IRA — from the Civil War, through the torturing of Stephen Hayes, through the split between Officials and Provisionals, to the more recent feuding inside the break-away INLA — are so bitter and so bloody. These matters have little to do with the usual concepts of democracy. As far as revolutionary armies, not backed by a government in power, are concerned, getting the British out of Ireland — or getting the Spanish presence out of Basqueland — has very little to do with the practice of counting heads without reference to what the heads contain. It has everything to do with letting as much fresh air as possible into as many as possible of the heads that constitute "legitimate targets". The campaign itself will be legitimised much later — as was the Rising of 1916, the War of Independence, and the Civil War — by political success which could not have been achieved without the military campaign. That this success has, so far in Ireland, brought further frustration and splits to the IRA matters not a whit to these who see themselves as the ones who will finally establish the elusive thirty-two-county Republic.

In a television interview, in the days before Section 31 of the Broadcasting Act, Máirtín O Cadhain gave an interesting insight into the relationship between the IRA and Sinn Féin in the 1940s. Stating that he was never a member of Sinn Féin, he said he found it amusing to be a prisoner in the Curragh Internment Camp, after the internees had burned the huts and Barney Casey had been shot in the back by soldiers who claimed he was charging towards them aggressively (the inquest on him was adjourned and never resumed after Seán MacBride asked one rather obvious question), and get the loan of an issue of the *Kerryman* from some Kerry prisoner in which he read the latest instalment in a long, acrimonious correspondence.

It was between two members of Sinn Féin, J. J. O'Kelly (Sceilg) and Brian O'Higgins, and the subject was the death of the prominent Republican priest from Sligo, Fr Michael O'Flanagan, who had done his very best to prevent de Valera from taking Sinn Féin away with him, holus bolus. Being as welcome as frost in August in his own diocese Fr O'Flanagan lived out the end of his life in frugal circumstances near Dublin. It seems that the rent of the house he lived in was paid, either directly or indirectly, by the Fianna Fáil Government.

Now the question under discussion was, did he die a true Republican or not? There was no easy answer to that important question, or was it that the answer was too easy? It is a tribute to Máirtín O Cadhain's sense of humour that he was able to appreciate the irony of the situation in the circumstances.

One of the more comforting of Irish left-wing myths, constantly encouraged by polemicists, amateur politicians, committed journalists and other inhabitants of that particular twilight zone, is that the IRA was capable of being transformed into an instrument of social and political reform. A small minority of members of the IRA harboured this desire at various times. The majority, not all of whom would be opposed to social and political change, believed that all this could wait until Ireland was free and its territory united.

Attempts were made to set a section of the IRA off on a different course. The Republican Congress of 1934, for instance, was an effort by Peadar O'Donnell, George Gilmore and others to form a revolutionary, left-wing alliance of industrial workers and small farmers. What these two groupings had in common, or what they would even talk about when they actually met, was a horse whose colour was certainly not red. Not that it mattered all that much as the Congress petered out rapidly. The attempts to give it a posthumous standing not enjoyed by it in its lifetime, are yet another example of the extraordinary capacity of the blindly committed to turn the footnotes of history into pages of text.

It may be good show-business, but it is scarcely good history.

In the 1960s and early 1970s another attempt was made to commit Sinn Féin and the IRA— before and after the split with the Provisionals in 1969— to an advanced socialist policy. The ground for this had been prepared by the *United Irishman* with its concentration on issues such as the ownership of Irish land and waters. This was a more serious attempt than any preceding one and for some years had been accompanied by the withdrawal of arms from the North. The destruction of capitalism, North and South, was the aim. Once that was accomplished it would be possible to unite Catholic and Protestant workers and establish an All-Ireland Republic of workers and small farmers and, presumably, the middle-class theorists who worked all this out.

The outbreak of real war in the North did a lot to retard this plan of campaign.

Some found it ironic, some downright funny, that many of the guns withdrawn from the North were sold to the Free Welsh Army: the first time in its history that the IRA had surplus arms for sale. To make matters even funnier the arms were subsequently recovered from the bottom of Lake Bala by British Army frogmen after a welshing of nerves on the part of their new owners.

One may easily be short of a job, a house, regular sex, drink (rarely) or food in Ireland: one is rarely short of the makings of a bitter belly-laugh.

But the war against capitalism in the South went on. Some foreign-owned farms in Meath and elsewhere were attacked with bombs, a foreign-owned trawler was blown up in Ros a' Mhíl harbour, and war was declared on an estate near Uachtar Ard which was being converted into a golf course. A man who is now a paragon of all the middle-class virtues was constantly available to direct television crews towards the area where the next "big bang" was likely to take place.

Unfortunately, the biggest one claimed the life of a young volunteer from Cork, Martin O'Leary, whose unit was trying to destroy an electricity transformer at Mogul Mines in north Tipperary. He was burned to death when the explosion went wrong. At his burial in Cork, in June 1971, the man who was then Chief-of-Staff of the Official IRA, Cathal Goulding, explained what this phase in the national struggle was all about and what its instruments were to be:

> Unfortunately it is not within our power to dictate what action the forces of imperialism and exploitation will engage in to repress, coerce, and deny ordinary people their God-given rights. When their answers to the just demands of the people are the lock-out, strike-breaking, eviction, coercion, the prison cell, intimidation or the gallows then our duty is to reply as he replied, in the language that brings these vultures to their senses most effectively — the language of the bomb and the bullet.

In ten years the language changed to the language of the ballot box, but don't all shout together about what happened the Army and its weaponry. First we must follow another bunch of reformed gunmen into Dáil Eireann.

Fianna Fáil, the Party of Reality — later dubbed the Gurrier Party by Myles na Gopaleen — was founded in Dublin in April 1926, and the first of its many All-Ireland Final-like Ard Fheiseanna was held in November. It made its mark immediately. It successfully hijacked the better part of the old Sinn Féin election machine and refurbished it. The IRA, while keeping their distance theoretically, supported it and even tried to arrange temporary electoral peace between the new party and Sinn Féin.

The Free State Government was becoming intensely

unpopular, because of its economic policies, high unemployment and the new repressive measures introduced by Kevin O'Higgins against subversives. The agreement signed by Ernest Blythe with the British Government on the payment of land annuities to Britain, was regarded as punitive and shameful. It was remarked that Blythe's capacity to flap his hands and scream, "Shoot them!" was considerably diminished when he faced British negotiators.

In the general election of June 1927, Fianna Fáil won forty-four seats, just two seats less than Cumann na nGael. Earlier in the year de Valera had recognised the Free State to the extent of applying for a passport to travel to the United States. Irish-American money was needed to sustain the new party and to found a daily newspaper it needed to get its message to the people.

The matter of getting into the Dáil, past the Cerberic oath, was still unresolved and the forty-four deputies and their leader feared the dreaded paralysis induced by abstentionism. De Valera was later to say that when he wanted to know what the Irish people wanted all he had to do was look into his own heart. A quick glance at Irish history in the nineteenth century would have been enough to tell him that the Irish people had struggled far too hard to achieve the right to vote to negate it by electing Republican angels who would dance on the heads of ideological pins in Limbo.

Dan Breen showed that there was a simple way into the Dáil by taking the oath and entering the chamber in January 1927, and shrugging off all the Republican flak that came his way. *An Phoblacht* lamented "that he should have overshadowed his other days by his crime".

Breen tried to introduce a bill to abolish the oath, this being the purpose of the exercise. But it now became obvious that the famous stepping-stones to full freedom had been covered by a flood of spite. Cosgrave was not having any of it. The oath was part of the Treaty and would so remain. De Valera and his followers would have to come in and swallow it, their pride, their principles and the cold cinders of the Civil War.

Kevin O'Higgins, Free State Minister for Justice and External Affairs, typically was the one to place the banderillas in de Valera's neck, branding him as "the man who did his damnedest to cut his country's throat and now invited it to commit political hari-kiri in order to save his face." That face-saving was involved was clear, but it was not all on one side as would become increasingly clear once Fianna Fáil were inside the Dáil.

Just as de Valera thought he had discovered a constitutional chink in the Free State's armour and was considering the possibility of challenging the validity of the oath in a referendum, everything changed suddenly. Kevin O'Higgins was gunned down near his home and died of his wounds later.

Although O'Higgins would have qualified for the title of Most Hated Minister, as much for his acid tongue as for the repressive legislation he put through the Dáil, the authorities did not have the slightest clue as to who his assassins might have been. Many were picked up but none were charged, and when the IRA issued a statement denying responsibility it was accepted that the killing had not been officially sanctioned.

Over the years many theories were advanced and one novel was based loosely on the killing. Dublin gallows humour had O'Higgins killed because he introduced the "Holy Hour" to the pubs in the Intoxicating Liquor Act of 1924. As the years passed it was not unusual to hear it murmured, after an Old-IRA-man's funeral, "Another of the men who shot O'Higgins gone! There's only a few of them left now." But since the publication of the autobiography of Harry White, *Harry,* in 1985, the names of those who carried out the killing are known: much to the embarrassment of those who had claimed this grisly national record for their own particular candidates.

What is still not clear, however, is how much of an accident the meeting of the four armed men in the stolen car, with Kevin O'Higgins on Booterstown Avenue, on a quiet Sunday morning, really was. It may be of only academic interest now, but it helps to keep curiosity about one of the strangest political assassinations of the century awake.

But what mattered very much to the development of Irish politics was the legislation put through the Dáil as a consequence of his assassination. Referenda were abolished and elected deputies not taking the oath within two months of their election would automatically forfeit their seats. At last Cosgrave had de Valera in a corner.

The circumstances of Fianna Fáil's entry to Dáil Eireann, in August 1927, are well known. De Valera signed the required book, having first removed the Bible that lay on it to the far end of the room, declaring loudly that he was taking no oath. A great man for the symbols was Dev!

Was it all as simple as that after the jigs and the theological reels and the Civil War? There has never been a final and definitive answer to that question. Those who believed that an oath had in effect been taken shouted, "Perjury!"; those who believed that old Houdini de Valera had sprung free from the trap the bloody-minded Free Staters had rigged for him shouted, "Empty Formula." That is still the situation whenever the matter is discussed with feeling.

What has been noticed, and not only by begrudgers but by every Justice and Judge sufficiently sober to be aware of what is going on in his court, is that there seems to be no respect at all for the oath in Ireland, and that this had been the case for years. They are swallowed daily, and not just by plaintiffs, defendants and witnesses but by members of the Garda Síochána as well, as if they were raw eggs and sherry. Indeed, in many parts of the country the only law practised in the District and Circuit Courts is summarised in the phrase: "You swear for me today and I'll swear for you tomorrow."

Whether or not the sleight of hand, heart and mind that occurred in the Clerk of the Dáil's office on that August day, can in any way be held responsible for this unwholesome state of affairs, we can only think aloud, our thoughts being conditioned by the company we happen to be in at the time.

Once inside the Dáil Fianna Fáil made its mark very rapidly and in alliance with Labour and some smaller parties, almost brought down the Government on a vote of no confidence. The Government was saved by the Ceann Comhairle's casting vote but had Deputy Jinks from Sligo not been "nobbled" and sent home on the train in an exceedingly tired condition, after a lot of free booze, Fianna Fáil would have scored its first parliamentary goal. But even as the country made jokes about the elusive Sligoman, with the euphonious name, Cosgrave called a general election anyway. Like the racehorse named after him Jinks had peaked too soon. He lost his seat in the election just as the horse, having won the Two Thousand Guineas, came a cropper in the Derby.

There is a rather hairy myth abroad that Cosgrave was such a deep believer in democracy that he greased a slipway into the Dáil for de Valera, past the hindering Testament. In fact he was anxious to have another election. The "nobbling" of Jinks was carried out by Major Bryan Cooper, an Independent Unionist TD, who was afraid of losing his own seat if the Government fell. He joined Cumann na nGael and saved it. John Jinks must have spent the remaining seven years of his life sticking pins in Cooper's effigy.

Cosgrave was sure that Fianna Fáil's funds were exhausted by the June election, and that the business of the oath would lose them the support of strict Republicans and all right-thinking Catholics. That was the kind of Ireland poor W. T. Cosgrave lived in. But he may well have been taking advice from clerics like the Dean of Cashel, Monsignor Ryan, who addressed the farmers at Cashel Fair and instructed them not to vote for a party that had reduced an oath in the name of God Almighty to a pantomime. It is interesting to note that Fianna Fáil actually won an extra seat in Tipperary.

Many priests gave similar advice from the pulpit. Masses in parts of the country were enlivened by walks-out during sermons and impromptu arguments between priests and Fianna Fáil supporters who refused to allow political sermons to go unanswered.

Not all of this was to Fianna Fáil's advantage. Because of their support for the socialist grouping Saor Eire, proscribed by the Government in 1931 as well as the IRA, the label "Communist" was attached to the new party. It must have been reasonably effective or Fianna Fáil would not have used it against the Labour Party so frequently in years to come.

But this conflict with the Catholic Church, as well as previous tussles during the Civil War, nurtured a type of Fenian anti-clericalism in many members of the new Fianna Fáil party. Dr Noel Browne, when he sought refuge in the Party of Reality until "Old Mischief" MacEntee had him booted out again, found that some of it still survived in the fifties among a handful of backbenchers. These men, of course, had not been debilitated by the power of ministerial office.

The election resulted in gains for the two big parties at the expense of Labour (even at this early stage being prepared for its role as the bridesmaid of Irish politics), the other small groupings and the Independents. Cumann na nGael gained fifteen seats, and Fianna Fáil thirteen, on the June returns. Cumann na nGael, with the help of the Farmers and most Independents, were able to form a precarious Government but one which ran its full term. De Valera was well pleased with his gains but even more pleased that Fianna Fáil retained every seat it won in the previous election. He took this as a vindication of his entry into the Dáil and evidence that the furore about the oath had done no great damage, certainly not in the rural areas where parish priests were supposed to have the power. Other interests needed further convincing and de Valera was alive to his areas of weakness.

He was not yet satisfied with the efficiency of the party

organisation, or its capacity to react to a general election called at short notice. He keenly felt the lack of a daily paper to explain party policies and give Cumann na nGael the lambasting Fianna Fáil was getting from every daily newspaper in the country at the time. This was a matter of urgency and money was raised at home and in America to launch a Republican paper. To ensure the purity and continuity of its Republicanism, control of the newspaper — and of the group of newspapers when it came about — was in the hands of the de Valera family, even into the farthest generations.

The *Irish Press* was launched in 1931 and met with aggressive official hostility from the start. A cartoon in *Dublin Opinion* captured one aspect of the hostility. It showed a reporter, notebook and pencil in hand, lying on his back on the pavement outside Government Buildings. A little old lady was looking down at him quizzically and the caption read:

"Banana-skin?"

"No! *Irish Press*."

The new daily paper, later to be christened *Pravda* by James Dillon, helped the party enormously. Not alone did it cater for the party faithful but it quickly gained readers who might not necessarily favour the paper's political line but who appreciated the quality of its news and sports coverage.

Many found it amusing that it was an Englishman, hired by de Valera as sports editor, who pioneered the exhaustive coverage of gaelic games in Irish newspapers. Not that this endeared either Joe Sherwood, or Eamon de Valera, to those who controlled the GAA. They suspected that de Valera was a rugby man at heart and Joe Sherwood was not a "True Gael" either, being an Englishman and an enterprising journalist who saw the unexploited potential of gaelic games. Indeed no less a person than the General Secretary of the GAA came into the paper's front office one day and asked to see the sports editor whom he proceeded to flatten with a punch because of his comments on matters the GAA wished to keep "in Lodge".

All this was to the good of the paper, of course, and it quickly became the country's second paper in terms of circulation. Adversity, short of actual censorship, never harmed a newspaper anyway. It usually helps to sharpen wits and comments and encourages writers to sail as close to the wind as the laws of libel and the courage of editors allow.

Party organisation was handled by a team under de Valera's personal supervision. There is a cultivated myth which would have us believe that de Valera won elections by putting on a big black cloak, appearing on platforms at twilight illuminated by blazing sods of turf, and casting spells on people in bad Irish.

The histrionics were a help in the days when election meetings were a form of open-air theatre with audience participation in the form of chants such as "Murderer", "Perjurer", "Spanish Bastard", "Seventy-Seven", "Who fed the birds at Ballyseedy?", often accompanied by sticks, stones, rotten eggs and fresh cow-dung, as well as periodic chargings of the police and the platform. Television may well have introduced the pleasures of sex to Ireland, as Oliver J. Flanagan discovered, but it took an awful lot of excitement out of electioneering: the heckler in the crowd was replaced by the creepy-crawly National Handler with the syrupy slogan.

Fianna Fáil produced two manuals, "Coras Bua" and "Bealach Bua", containing hardly any Irish, apart from their titles, but packed with practical advice. It is thought that de Valera contributed much of the detail.

"Bealach Bua" deals with all the activities, social and political, of Fianna Fáil Cumainn, except those concerned directly with the conduct of an election campaign. This is dealt with in the fifty pages of "Coras Bua". Part of the instructions to tallymen at the counting centres gives a flavour of the whole:

He must realise that an election can be lost through "sharp" practice and trickery and he should be ever watchful to ensure that the votes and preferences given our Candidates are not — by accident or design — credited to our opponents. He should take up a position opposite one of the officials appointed to check and count the papers and should try to keep an accurate tally of Fianna Fáil votes in each box dealt with by that official. He should not, out of curiosity or otherwise, leave his post to see what goes on elsewhere. His job is to stay put — not to ramble. Above all he should not take intoxicants during the day.

Canvassing, cross-checks on earlier canvasses, lists of wavering supporters, local and national publicity, transport, finance, sample ballot-papers, the workings of proportional representation, election law, insurance coverage for drivers and passengers on polling day, and the conduct of public meetings are all dealt with in the same detailed fashion. This extract bears the authentic stamp of de Valera's life-long devotion to the essential dull details of how the bottom rung of the ladder to power is hammered into place:

The uncertainty of our climate makes it imperative to study the comfort of the audience by siting the platform in the most sheltered spot available. Never use the centre of a large open square where even a big crowd looks small. Stay a reasonable distance from the Church (if there is one in the vicinity) to avoid disturbing worshippers. Resist the temptation to hold the meeting near a cross no matter how attractive the position. Remember that reporters need light, if it is an afternoon meeting, and provide accordingly. Platform essentials are a sufficient number of chairs, a table for the press, and an effective microphone. Most vital of all — there must be a banner, streamer, or large poster prominently displayed showing in bold type the words Fianna Fáil and the names of the candidates. Great care should be exercised to avoid disrespect in the use of the National Flag.

With all this and the formidable backing of the IRA (Fianna Fáil and that banned organisation marched together in Bodenstown in 1931), to ensure that canvassing was carried out with due emphasis on essentials, and that the emigrants, the dead and others unavoidably absent, voted early and often, Fianna Fáil went into the election campaign of 1932 in good heart.

Cumann na nGael put its trust in the established Free State families, businessmen, big farmers, their best-known leaders and the Press, excluding the brash newcomer, and the old reliable Law and Order. Then, on the eve of the election, the Government was possessed of a death-wish. Ernest Blythe was the first to indicate the presence of suicidal tendencies when he reduced old age pensions by a shilling in a special pre-election Budget.

Just in case that did not do the trick the *Irish Press* was prosecuted for seditious libel and its editor hauled before the Military Tribunal.

Fianna Fáil won seventy-two seats to become the biggest party in the Dáil, but without an overall majority. With the support of Labour, who had become thoroughly exasperated with Cumann na nGael's refusal to implement any of the social legislation outlined in the Democratic Programme of the First Dáil, and three Independents, Fianna Fáil formed its first Government.

There were rumours of a possible Free State Army coup, and a whole folklore has grown up about the guns some of the Fianna Fáil deputies carried into Leinster House that day, but everything passed off quietly. Having worked so hard to back de Valera and his party into the House, Cumann na nGael could hardly try to back them out again. Before long they were going to find themselves confronting the new Government in extraparliamentary activity all dressed up in their nice blue shirts and black tams.

6

"Ireland was a nation when England was a pup"

No sooner had de Valera named his first Cabinet than he dispatched two of them to Arbour Hill Prison to greet the IRA prisoners who had been sentenced by the Military Tribunal. It was noticed that the Minister for Defence, Frank Aiken, who was accompanied by the Minister for Justice, James Geoghegan, was on Christian name terms with most of the senior prisoners; which was not all that strange when one considers that he was their Chief of Staff a short time previously.

Fianna Fáil had already been in touch with Seán MacBride, a member of the Army Council of the IRA, to find out if all the prisoners had been acting under orders from the Council, or if some of them had been off on solo-runs. The day after the ministerial visitation all prisoners were released.

In the course of his first contacts with IRA leaders de Valera gave signs, had there been attentive ears to note them, that he was running in a different set of tracks to those the IRA had laid for him. He made vague references to renegotiating the Treaty on the basis of Document No. 2 (a piece of de Valera verbal atom-splitting, in 1922, which need not detain us here) and not being able to see a clear role for their Army now that Frank Aiken was in charge of the one to which he surrendered in 1923, but had not really surrendered, for the IRA now had the guns dumped on his instructions.

It was obvious that de Valera was having a good look at those stepping stones with the stronger of his two eyes and turning the other one on his important but most uncomfortable allies.

They were in a state of absolute euphoria. Maud Gonne MacBride exclaimed, "Ireland has stood together on this. The IRA stood firm and they have defeated Cosgrave and the coercionists." She did not have to draw attention to the fact that the IRA used a strange constitutional instrument to bring this about. She was speaking in a form of shorthand, not unknown in our own time, by which a minority assumes another mantle and pretends to be a majority. Like all the better Irish political tricks it is essentially verbal.

Moss Twomey, Chief of Staff of the IRA, did not use shorthand when he delivered the Army Council's message to the troops at the 1916 Commemoration that year. He clearly enunciated what was to become the IRA's principal justification for its continued existence. The message stated that the small and at the time unrepresentative body of armed men who effected the Rebellion of 1916 had established the right and the authority of the Irish nation to fight for its right to inalienable sovereign independence. Those with long memories remembered that a very prominent Republican leader said something very like that to justify the continuation of the armed struggle in 1922. Those who agreed but mildly with the sentiments gave thanks to God that this sainted personage was now in charge of the affairs of state and that all would have to be right on the night. Those who were beginning to believe that Republican lightning always struck twice rubbed their hands and waited for the bell to start the next round.

But as far as the new Government was concerned the IRA could wait. It was careful not to remove too many of the hated Special Branch officers from their positions as the IRA resumed drilling and carried out some retaliatory forays of their own. De Valera knew that he would yet need the political police — who knew the location of areas of sensitivity both militaristic and anatomical — just as he might still need the lads with the unofficial guns and use them, provided they did not prod him too often in the ribs with demands for a real, live, thirty-two-county Republic.

Getting rid of some of the useless stepping stones and giving a new aspect to others was not a matter of urgency. The detested oath would have to go, so would the Governor General, the Land Annuities, the British military presence in Spike Island, Bearhaven and Lough Swilly ... and then there was the little matter of uniting Ireland; not to mention domestic matters such as unemployment, emigration, the revival of the ancestral language and getting Fianna Fáil the kind of parliamentary majority which would rid them of troublesome supporters not of the true faith.

The oath was abolished, to all intents and purposes, by putting a Bill to abolish it through the Dáil. The Senate refused to pass it and by so doing passed sentence of death on itself. Then the Governor-General was dumped. Tim Healy had by this time gone to join the Fenians and Bishop Moriarty in heaven and the job was being done by a decent poor man called James McNeill. He was not up to the role in which he found himself — the pebble in de Valera's constitutional shoe.

Having been snubbed on a few occasions and publicly humiliated during the Eucharistic Congress, McNeill went public with his grievances. The Government then asked the British Government and the King to get rid of him, while refusing to state reason or cause, and as the request was within the terms of the Treaty, McNeill had to go.

He was replaced by one Dónal O Buachalla, a 1916 veteran from Maynooth, who lived in a suburban house in Dublin, signed whatever was put in front of him, attended no official functions and wore heavy tweed suits whenever he went out of doors. He was not even called the Governor-General but An Seanascal, an esoteric term from Old God's time which was irreverently translated into English as "The Old Armpit". He most certainly could not have been classified as "gentry".

The Land Annuities were a far more serious matter than the oath — which was well and truly an empty formula at this stage — or the office of Governor-General, for the Annuities were draining some of the state's substance.

The Annuities were the sums the farmers paid annually to the British Government to repay loans raised to buy out the landlords between 1891 and 1909. Because of the Troubles they had not been collected for some years but after the Ultimate Financial Settlement, signed by Winston Churchill and Ernest Blythe in great secrecy in 1926, these payments and others, covering pensions for members of the RIC, were being levied on farmers who, as well as being as reluctant to pay anything in the wide world to the state at any time, were genuinely in bad circumstances. The international slump in trade had hit farmers, large and small, and the Annuities amounted to five million pounds a year.

Peadar O'Donnell saw the situation as God's gift to left-wing politics, as well as an opportunity to spancel Fianna Fáil to the IRA's left leg. It took him some time to convince de Valera to take up the issue as part of the election campaign of 1932, but once committed to the agitation de Valera snatched it from O'Donnell, and turned it inside out and upside down to the maximum benefit of Fianna Fáil. It was this experience that caused O'Donnell to advise his followers later on to join Fianna Fáil and endeavour to wheel it towards more radical causes from inside.

Although he could never bring himself to abandon his own peculiar cloak and dagger brand of politics, Peadar O'Donnell was realistic enough to see that some issues called for the backing of the big battalions. He had first offered the Land Annuities as a cause to the Labour Party. They regretfully turned it down as they feared the "Red" smear which they knew would follow from the pulpits of Ireland. Labour was now waiting, on its hands and knees.

The British Government could not have been expected to accept any one of the three measures adopted by the new Irish Free State Government without protesting that the

Treaty was being dismantled. This they did and when they got no satisfaction they retaliated by imposing punitive taxes on Irish exports to Britain. Because these taxes mainly affected Irish agricultural produce it is sometimes thought that they were a result of the refusal to pay the Land Annuities. In fact the Economic War, as this incident became known, was caused by the three steps back from the Treaty of 1922.

The Cumann na nGael party in opposition did itself further damage by being so appreciative of the British position. Its attitude was that the Treaty was being dishonoured and that this was a shameful thing. Ernest Blythe declared that his signature on the financial agreement was being dishonoured also. It was also said truly that the farmers were going to suffer — particularly the big cattle-raising farmers who voted Cumann na nGael and who were now flocking into the Blueshirts.

What was strange about the Cumann na nGael position was that while in Government Cosgrave and his ministers were exploiting the stepping stone theory of the Treaty, stealthily, by joining international organisations like the League of Nations independently of Britain. But when de Valera began to demonstrate that the stepping stones might lead away from the King altogether the opposition could only call "Foul".

One could understand their fury at hearing de Valera admit that the Treaty was capable of even greater flexibility than he ever imagined. His remark caused others to mutter that it was a great pity that such hindsight could not raise the dead to life. Those who kept a cool head at the time — and one would expect a degree of healthy cynicism from the 100,000 unemployed — would certainly have good reason to worry about the country's future in the light of the confusion being caused by its recent past.

With de Valera in charge, however, they may still have lacked jobs but certainly not excitement. In one of his fits of calculated pique he called a general election for January 1933.

Most of his ministers thought him mad. With years of hindsight Seán Lemass alone claims credit for having been in on the plan and also having spurred de Valera on. The ministers were summoned, one by one, and told that he had taken the decision on his own and would stand or fall by it.

He had his reasons. The arrangement with the Labour Party was breaking down and he needed an overall majority to deal with the British Government, the farmers who were organising angrily, the Blueshirts who were encouraging them, and the Senate which he was going to abolish for trying to trip him up. The IRA was sweetened with unspoken understandings of heads to be lopped off for previous bad behaviour, if the Government was strong enough to wield the axe.

The election was as bitter as the weather. All the opposition could promise was to undo what de Valera and Fianna Fáil had already done. This was more bad medicine. The people had now been given a cause and were not interested in backward looks. But de Valera took the Cumann na nGael attitude as a form of treason. He blamed Cosgrave, whom he despised, and there is no evidence that the two men ever exchanged a word, outside of formal Dáil business, for the rest of their lives.

Fianna Fáil won its first overall majority. Dev's quick look into his heart to read the wishes of the people had paid off. It was also a triumph for Seán Lemass, once again director of elections, to disprove once more the myth that Dubliners cannot understand the mysteries of life beyond the Dead Man Murray's on the Lucan Road.

Fianna Fáil got almost fifty per cent of the votes cast to Cumann na nGael's thirty-one per cent. Significantly, Fianna Fáil almost doubled its vote in Dublin on its 1927 figures. If Labour had eyes to see they could glimpse the Dublin working classes sliding down Fianna Fáil's gullet after the small farmers of the western seaboard. It was hardly the Republican Congress scenario but it was reality.

With the election behind him de Valera gave substance to one unspoken promise and fired the Commissioner of the Garda Síochána, General Eoin O'Duffy, without telling him or anyone else why it had to be done. Fianna Fáil developed a knack of its own when it came to abolishing head men. The IRA knew that they had been demanding this with bended trigger-fingers, if not on bended knees, and they were well pleased. They were also pleased that Civil War military service was to qualify members for military pensions, but not so pleased that some overjoyed members were joining the regular army and the Garda Síochána. There were times when the IRA believed in keeping its distance.

Two relics of this winter election were, until more recent times, to be seen on two rock-faces in de Valera's own constituency of Clare. One was a simple statement of fact:

Ireland was a Nation when England was a pup
And Ireland will be a Nation when England is buggered up.

The other was connected with the Economic War and a suggestion of de Valera's that instead of importing tea at vast expense Ireland should brew its own light beer, thus creating many jobs and saving a lot of money. The idea was not to the liking of one slogan-writer who wrote:

WE WANT NO LIGHT BEER

to which another more positive thinker added:

NO: GIVE US GOOD STRONG PORTER.

De Valera was now forced to turn his attention to the Blueshirts. Founded in 1931 as the Army Comrades Association, under the leadership of Dr T. F. O'Higgins, brother of Kevin, it seemed at first to be a benevolent society but gradually changed its appearance and its objectives. By the end of 1932 it had 100,000 members, had adopted a Fascist-style uniform of blue shirt and black tam (blue blouse in the case of its ladies' and little girls' sections) and salute. At first it floundered around in search of something akin to a philosophy and a leader with more charisma than Dr O'Higgins who bore a remarkable resemblance to a baked cod-fish. The arrival of General O'Duffy, with the mark of the Beast still fresh on his posterior, gave the movement the spiritual momentum it needed and in August 1933, O'Duffy announced that a huge convergence on Dublin, to honour Collins, Griffith and O'Higgins, would take place later in the month. Tens of thousands of Blueshirts would take part. Needless to say, many people — and not alone supporters of Fianna Fáil and the IRA — immediately thought of Mussolini's March on Rome.

The Blueshirts were about many things, continental Fascism being one of the least of them. In their own little tin-pot way they were an Irish solution to various Irish problems of the day. But they were far from being the jolly, rather silly lot of amateur actors in fancy dress that some contemporary historians would wish us to believe. There was a rather unpleasant stain on the tail of the Blueshirt as we shall see.

Initially they were an attempt to fight the Civil War all over again by taking on Fianna Fáil and the IRA in a peculiar form of role-reversal. Then there was the matter of freedom of speech. Some maintain that they were organised to guarantee freedom of speech to Cumann na nGael speakers whose meetings were being broken up by the IRA who were beginning to feel their Republican (Fianna Fáil trademarked) oats.

Frank Ryan had summed up the IRA attitude succinctly: "No matter what anyone says to the contrary, while we have fists, hands and boots to use, and guns if necessary, we will not allow free speech to traitors." Instead of "Traitor" others used "Fascist".

On the other hand one reads that the Blueshirts went around denying free speech to others on the grounds that they "did not support the view that communists should be free to organise". This anti-communistic crusade made the movement popular with many of the clergy. Communism, Republicanism and Sexual Licence (which meant an impure thought which remained in occupation for more than five seconds) were the Irish sins that cried out to the Bishops in those years.

To indicate what the atmosphere of the country was like at the time the following quotations may prove helpful. The first is from an editorial in the Cumann na nGael newspaper, *United Irishman,* in December 1932:

> Whatever his [de Valera's] intentions may have been, or may now be, he is proceeding along the Bolshevik path almost as precisely as if he was getting daily orders from Moscow. His government is unmistakably out to demoralise the police force, and render them incapable of dealing with armed terrorists. His financial policy is leading inevitably to despolitary taxation, which, rounded off with a dose of inflation, may be trusted to dispose of our Irish Kulaks.

The next is from one of those great Irish institutions of the past, the Confirmation Sermon. This one was given by another Bishop of Galway, Dr O'Doherty, referred to by many charitable commentators as "eccentric" which may be construed in more modern parlance as "tired *and* emotional". In May 1933, he came to warn his flock in Kinvara against joining secret and suspect societies. His Lordship took this interesting lurch through a segment of Irish history:

> Who fought in '98? Was it the United Irishmen? It was not; it was the men of Meath and Wexford who fought. What about the men of '48? They hatched a cabbage garden plot. What did Emmet do? He led a rabble through the streets of Dublin. The same applied to '67. Who went out in 1916? Who faced the Black and Tans in this country? Was it any of the secret societies? It was not: it was the decent young men of the country. What

did cut-throat Tone do? We hear a lot about these people, and they are held up as heroes, so called heroes; but secret societies or those who belonged to them were never of any benefit to the country.

This speech, for it could hardly qualify as a sermon, would have passed unnoticed had not Galway County Council almost completed the building of a new bridge across the Corrib, near Claddagh. It would have probably been named Claddagh Bridge had not the Bishop's reference to Wolfe Tone annoyed the Fianna Fáil and Republican majority on the council so much that the bridge was named Wolfe Tone Bridge.

The Bishop was not amused, nor was the parish priest in Kerry who was so carried away in his praise for the Blueshirts and their mode of dress that he admitted to a temptation: he felt like donning one himself. To his surprise and annoyance his remark earned a warm response from a woman in the congregation who called out: "Go on, Father, sure mightn't it suit you a lot better than that auld black one you have to wear."

The third offering is taken from the first issue of the Blueshirt's own paper, *The Blueshirt*, which contained detailed plans for the great parade in Dublin. It also carries a denial that the organisation is a Fascist one: "The Fenians, the Land League, the Gaelic League, the Volunteers and Sinn Féin made the tradition out of which the National Guard has sprung.... " Then it goes on to deal with the accusation that it is anti-Semite:

I suppose there are not many who are silly enough to believe that the National Guard is Nazi or anti-Semite. It is true that the new Constitution confines membership to Irishmen who profess the Christian Faith. But what is expressed in the new Constitution, in this respect, was unmistakably implied in the old Constitution. The Constitution adopted by the ACA last February bound its members to uphold Christian principles and oppose alien control and influence in National affairs.

While stating that there is no evidence that the Blueshirts were in any way anti-Semitic as the Mosleyites in Britain were, Maurice Manning in his book *The Blueshirts* goes on to say:

> The only nagging doubt on this question arises in connection with the proviso in the constitution of the National Guard which confined membership of the movement to "those of Irish birth or parentage who profess the Christian Faith". No explanation for this proviso was ever offered. It may possibly have been designed to keep Jews out, or it may more probably have been a bit of pious rhetoric.

Anti-Semitism in Ireland, such as it was, is difficult to trace into the open. Nobody ever, to my knowledge, put up a notice in Dublin to the effect that members of the Jewish faith better set up their own golf club if they wished to play regularly, but that is what happened. Smears are no less effective for being whispered and de Valera was once moved to speak in a most uncharacteristic way in public concerning his own antecedents. He was replying to an opposition-inspired smear that he was the bastard son of a Spanish Jew:

> There is not, so far as I know, a single drop of Jewish blood in my veins. On both sides I come from Catholic stock. My father and mother were married in a Catholic Church on September 19th 1881. I was born in October 1882. I was baptised in a Catholic church. I was brought up here in a Catholic home.

One wonders why cries of "Briscoe the Jewman" were heard so often at Blueshirt meetings when the deteriorating state of the country was mentioned. Captain Quish, a prominent Limerick Blueshirt, once accused the Government of being "a crowd of Spaniards, Jews and Manxmen". The Jew here was not de Valera but Seán Lemass who was reputed by the whispered smear to have been in hock to the Dublin Jewish bookmakers the Mirrelsons. This was broadly hinted at when he was appointed Taoiseach, by James Dillon and Joe Blowick.

The Blueshirts were probably appealing to the same constituency which the following extract from an article in *Fiat* was aimed at in 1956. This paper was published by an organisation which stood for the Cause of the Social Rights of Christ the King:

> On June 25, 1956, a Jew was elected for the first time in history as Lord Mayor of Dublin. In the assembly of town councillors at which he was elected, Catholics predominated but were divided in political allegiance. On the main issue before them, however — that of electing a Lord Mayor for the Catholic capital of Ireland — they were as one in ensuring that the reproach of what is known and feared in Ireland as intolerance should not be levelled at the proceedings. In point of fact, the election of a Jew as Lord Mayor of Dublin has been exemplified as a noteworthy instance of freedom from bigotry.
>
> The truth of the matter is that God's torn Hands and Feet, God's drawn Face, God's scourged and wounded body, glistening with the sweat of Death upon the Cross, if not totally forgotten, exercised precious little influence on these proceedings of the Catholic town councillors of Dublin. Not one voice questioned the fitness of a Catholic city having as its first citizen a member of a Nation that rejects the Divinity of Christ.

The Blueshirts drew back from the confrontation in Dublin, after the great parade was proscribed. It was just as well, for not alone was there a strong force of Gardaí and soldiers on duty but a strong auxiliary force of IRA-men were placed in strategic positions ready and able to mow down the marchers. They must have been terribly disappointed to have missed official "unofficial" action.

After that it was only a question of time until O'Duffy's megalomania, combined with his vanity and total brainlessness, wrecked the movement. The amazing part of that story is that he dominated so many men who liked to think of themselves as tough, bright and rather ruthless: men like Blythe, Mulcahy, McGilligan, MacEoin, T. F. O'Higgins and Commandant Cronin. He also managed to take over Fine Gael on its foundation, or rather it was handed to him. In the end he became an embarrassment, as did indeed the blueshirts and the tams and the salutes. Cosgrave took over as leader of the party and O'Duffy went off to raise a Brigade to fight for Franco in Spain.

The comic history of that escapade must be written one day: recruits armed with letters from their doctors saying that the Spanish climate would work miracles for their tubercular lungs: boys going to a dance in Dundalk from Carrickmacross and waking up on the *Dún Aengus* in Galway Bay the next day on their way to fight in Spain; O'Duffy having to inspect a guard of honour without weapons in case they shot him; the money collected to defend God in Spain being diverted to found a political dynasty; and finally, more men returning from Spain, despite the casualties inflicted on the Brigade by Franco's Moorish troops, than actually enlisted . . .

It may all have been concealed in a corner of that first issue of *The Blueshirt* in a ballad called "A President's Soliloquy" to be sung to the air, "The Pride of Petravore". One verse will suffice.

Hold the tide with pitchfork and with shovel;
Stop the restiveness that's bitin' at the people.
Shirts go chasin' backwards up the ceilin',
And licences are comin' home to roost.
Call the guards, and bid them snaffle Blythe —
Blythe's a bally gunman in disguise. . . .
Duffy too! he's dangerous at large. . . .
Clap the pair of 'em in clink this very night!

Chorus:
Woe's the day! my head is gone astray!
Ev'rything is blue! I think I have the flu!
Blue Shirts light around my bed at night.
And at dawn they dance a fling in Leinster Lawn!

The IRA had much better songs and were consequently much more of a real threat to de Valera and in the end proved impossible to get rid of, despite their own best efforts coupled with Fianna Fáil's use of Military Tribunals, firing squads, Mr Pierpoint the Hangman, internment without trial, the beating of prisoners by Special Branch officers who were once in the IRA themselves *after* the Civil War, allowing prisoners to die on hunger strike.... all the paraphernalia of the repressive Free State régime in the south and the Orange régime in the north.

7

Letitia Dunbar–Harrison's adventures with Páidín in the snipe grass

If the IRA suspected that it was being sized up for the long drop it showed no signs of it. Instead of finding out what further use de Valera had for it, the organisation behaved as if it had the Government under its control. An ultimatum was given, in all seriousness, to establish a real thirty-two-county Republic in five years or else. . . . It was clear that what was to follow, in the event of failure, was immediate and terrible war.

De Valera must have been as bewildered as most other observers by the campaign conducted by the IRA for the next decade; not that it got between him and his desire to rid the country of the illegal army, once and for all. It struck out in many directions simultaneously, getting involved in industrial and agrarian disputes and carrying out a series of shootings, calculated to inflict as much damage on the IRA as it did on the victims.

In 1936 the Government declared the IRA an illegal organisation and threw the Chief of Staff in Jail. The Military Tribunal, suspended by Fianna Fáil in 1932 to placate the IRA — as well as being offended by its anti-democratic nature — and revived to deal with the Blueshirts, was now used with full ferocity against the IRA.

Three shootings led to the declaration of illegality, which was never again revoked. Roderick More O'Farrell was shot dead in his house near Edgesworthtown, Co Longford, in 1935. His killing was not sanctioned by the

Army Council but it proved that if loaded guns are carried by nervous men they are more than likely to go off and kill anyone in their vicinity. This is as true of the official guns as it is of the unofficial ones.

The IRA had intervened in a dispute between tenants and the landlord over rent. A local unit had planned to tar and feather the elder More O'Farrell but shooting started and his son was killed. Although some men were charged with the killing the case was withdrawn from the jury, before the defence opened, because of an amazing muddle concerning identification. The men could thank their stars that a technical error had landed them in an ordinary court and not in the Military Tribunal.

The killing of Vice-Admiral Somerville, in early 1936, was not sanctioned either, but he too ended up very dead on the doorstep of his house in Castletownshend, in West Cork. A party of IRA-men had instructions to "put manners" on the elderly ex-naval officer who had been giving local lads, who had no prospect of employment at home, letters of recommendation for acceptance in the Royal Navy. As happened in many instances since, the orders "went wrong". The shooting of a man who was doing no more than the corporal works of mercy, stunned people in all parts of the country.

The killing of young John Egan, himself an IRA volunteer, in Dungarvan a month later horrified them. This was an official killing as Egan was suspected of having informed on his comrades. He was gunned down in full view of everyone in the street where he lived. Four men were charged with the shooting and one of them, Michael Conway, one of the best-known IRA-men in Munster, was sentenced to death. He was later released after a legal battle and became a monk in a contemplative order.

The Government moved with alacrity and with every appearance of delight at having been presented with such good excuses. Before long men were dying on hunger strike and the Garda Síochána were batoning crowds after funerals. *An Phoblacht*, until it was suppressed, used many of the old anti-Free State epithets, as well as some original ones, in its attacks on the new Free Staters.

The Army Council then decided that it was time to give the home front a rest and renew hostilities with the real enemy. It declared war on Britain and a bombing campaign was launched in various major cities. In August 1939, a bomb went off in the centre of Coventry killing five people. Two men, Peter Barnes and James McCormack, were sentenced to death and hanged on very flimsy evidence. But public hysteria had to be met with dramatic action — as seems to have been the case again with the Birmingham bombing during the current campaign in Britain.

Brendan Behan, who was involved in the campaign, appeared in court in another part of England on the day of the executions and has left a moving account of the experience in *Borstal Boy*.

For a few brief days Ireland went into mourning for the two men but more pressing matters nearer home occupied most peoples' minds: war had broken out and the Irish Government had opted for neutrality. The IRA declared for the old slogan "England's difficulty is Ireland's opportunity" and embarked on a "German Connection" which was nothing short of comic. But the organisation also showed that it had not lost all its resourcefulness. It emptied the Magazine Fort in the Phoenix Park of all its ammunition, including that for which the IRA had no suitable guns.

The coup was made easier by the fact that the senior IRA officer who planned it was employed in the Department of Defence. The raid was too successful and not enough dumping places were prepared, with the result that the Gardaí recovered more ammunition than was actually stolen.

The daring nature of the raid, more than its practical success, stung the Government into stern action. The Special Branch sought out every known suspect and the Curragh was filled with a variety of subversives. One of them, the hockey correspondent of a Dublin newspaper, who was lifted in error in place of a Protestant subversive from Kildare with a similar name, was ejected from the Camp in tears some days later. He had fallen in love with his new role in neutral Ireland.

The Military Tribunal — staffed mainly by officers from Northern Ireland, it was rumoured — was soon handing down sentences of death by the new-time. At first these sentences were carried out by firing squads of military policemen, in either Mountjoy or Portlaoise Prisons. Richard Goss from Dundalk was taken from Mountjoy to Portlaoise to be executed in this fashion, accompanied by an armed guard and the coffin in which he was to be buried in the prison grounds.

Furious that the IRA still insisted on shooting gardaí and Irish soldiers as part of the war effort, de Valera decided to do an Ernest Blythe and take the spurious glamour out of death by firing squad.

He brought over Pierpoint to hang Maurice O'Neill and Charlie Kerins. Republicans said that at least Blythe would have attempted to find a hangman who would be able to ask the victim in Irish if the knot was tickling his ear. In fact, had they known it, the Government had had an offer some years previously from a fluent Irish speaker for the job of Irish hangman. The letter of application was as follows:

Sir,
Since I am informed that there is a demand for a man (or woman) of Irish birth to fill the office of hang-man (or -woman) to the Irish Free State, I beg to state that I shall be ready at any time to take up work in this capacity, as there appear to be no other openings for young men of good family and liberal views in the Twenty-Six Counties. As I understand that the clothes, no longer required by the executed subject, form part of the perquisites of the office, this should incidentally solve — in a fashion — not the least of the problems confronting the father of a family since the launching of

our Government's "economic war". I beg to add that my piece-work rate for the execution of political malefactors would be lower than for persons driven to crime by economic need, as the work would be naturally less irksome (and the clothes of better quality). I may mention that as a translator of Gaelic poetry I should hope to pass the bilingual test, necessary for all appointments in the Free State, and doubtless essential for taking down the last remarks of prisoners, which are made, presumably, in Irish only. It will no doubt be a deep satisfaction to those homicides who have tasted public office and dignity to know that they are being hanged by a gentleman — a satisfaction which will be entirely mutual.

The applicant was Arland Ussher, translator of, among other poems, "Cúirt an Mheán Oíche", who, although he questioned the wisdom of the Economic War was in favour of de Valera's ideal of a largely self-supporting Ireland. However, he also believed that there should never have been a bullet fired in Ireland "from 1916 downward" as he put it in his book, *The Face and Mind of Ireland*. He sent his letter of application to the newspapers, not one of which published it.

The IRA was now in such a state of bewilderment that a group from the Northern Command, led by Seán McCaughey, came to Dublin to find out why so many things were going wrong. They concluded that there was a spy in their midst and decided that it was the Chief of Staff, Stephen Hayes, a Wexfordman with a weakness for drink. Dealing as he was with some very puritanical, not to mention single-minded, men his fondness for that which destroyed the chances of the men of '98 — among many others — did him no good at all.

With the aid of lighted cigarettes, chains and regular beatings his interrogators forced him to confess that he was giving information about the IRA to various Fianna Fáil ministers. Then he was told to write a full "Confession", after sentence of death was passed on him. He had the wit to take as long as he possibly could over the writing, while his captors discussed the time and manner of his execution. At one stage they were going to dump his body in front of Leinster House on the eve of the All-Ireland football final: a suggestion fraught with a macabre symbolism as Hayes had been a Wexford county footballer.

He managed to escape before the writing was finished, and just as the IRA was running out of safe houses, and arrived in Rathmines Garda Station in chains seeking sanctuary.

Subsequent events did little to bear out the contents of the "Confession". For every member of the IRA who believed even part of it there was another who saw it as an attempt to load the ills of an organisation in decline on a weak but honest man. Even the Internment Camp was riddled with dissent and bitterness.

When Charlie Kerins was arrested, in one of the last safe houses in Dublin, although its telephone was tapped and he was aware of it, he did not seem to have the will to stay on the run any longer. (It is a measure of the durability of the strange relationship between a certain element in Fianna Fáil and the IRA, even at this extreme stage, that Dan Breen's house in Tipperary was used as a safe house by men with death sentences hanging over them, as Harry White relates, even though Breen was a Fianna Fáil TD.)

Charlie Kerins had at this stage become Chief of Staff and his rank was to be his death warrant. There was no evidence to link him directly with the fatal shooting in ambush of Detective Denis O Brien, an ex-IRA-man drafted into the Garda Síochána by Fianna Fáil to keep an eye on anti-IRA and anti-Fianna Fáil detectives, and who was now on the IRA's death list for ill-treating its members in custody. It was assumed, in so far as a Military Tribunal needed justification for its decisions, that the Chief of Staff would have sanctioned the shooting and Kerins was hanged.

In Dáil Eireann Dan Spring raised his voice

courageously against the hanging, and was removed from the Chamber. The O'Rahilly football club in Tralee added "Kerins" to its title, but the *Kerryman*'s story of the disturbances in the town on the day of his execution was censored.

It looked to be the end of one Irish institution. Few could disagree with what the Minister for Justice, Gerry Boland, claimed to be the case: the IRA was dead and he had helped to kill it. As the haggard, dispirited internees came out of the Curragh in dribs and drabs, glad to get work from Tod Andrews clamping turf in the Phoenix Park for Bord na Móna, only a fool would have put a bent cent on the chances of the IRA ever again being a force in the political life of Ireland, north or south.

Before considering de Valera's Economic War, his new Constitution, the Anglo-Irish Agreement of 1938, neutrality in the World War and all that followed, it is as well to outline the ideals he and his party set out to achieve. Fianna Fáil aimed at:

> ... restoring the unity of Ireland and securing its independence, at placing as many families as possible on the land so that the food we eat, the clothes we wear, the houses we live in, and the articles in common daily use in the lives of our people may all, as far as is reasonably possible be produced by Irish labour from Irish material. Ireland united, Ireland free, Ireland self-supporting and self-reliant, Ireland speaking her own tongue and through it giving to the world the ancient treasures of Christian Gaelic culture — these are the ideals.

It is possible to stop and cry "Total failure" as many times as one feels necessary at this point, but events have a habit of moving on with little reference to the ideals that try to keep up with them.

The Economic War had become a very pressing matter which was inextricably mixed up with de Valera's con-stitutional re-adjustment. This, in turn, was connected with Partition and with the more pressing matter of the three British-held naval bases. This part of the Treaty of 1922 truly undermined the sovereignty of the Free State although Erskine Childers was the only member of the London delegation who made a fuss about it at the time.

The Economic War affected all farmers but particularly the big cattlemen. The scheme for slaughtering calves to prevent an even greater glut of beef on the market has truly entered the realm of folklore: the Holy Innocents of the Kine. But in one Gaeltacht area a ballad was composed in praise of de Valera because of the other scheme which provided dole-drawing families with a quota of free beef each week. Fianna Fáil turned its unwanted beef mountain to good electoral advantage.

Seán O'Faoláin in his short biography of de Valera, sadly out of print for many years, summed up the political effect of the Economic War on the Fianna Fáil leader, in this anecdote from Clare.

An old-age pensioner went into her local shop to buy groceries on a Friday. The shopkeeper drew her attention to the fact that a certain item was going to cost her a few pence more because of the Economic War. That was the latest blow her precious de Valera had inflicted on her, he sneered, but if there was an election in the morning she was probably fool enough to vote for him again.

"I would vote for him," said the old lady fiercely. "I would vote for him if it meant having to starve."

It was this capacity to inspire blind loyalty in people by appealing to their genuine patriotism, even when he was doing it all with mirrors, that makes de Valera such an uncomfortable figure in Irish politics.

Because it was all dovetailed into a highly-professional political machine which was all about the grasping and holding of power and was greatly at variance with the leader's rhetoric. As we can now clearly see, the machine gathered a momentum of its own with the passage of time. Its inner workings and smooth running became all-important and an end in itself. Gradually under Lemass, and finally under Lynch, a lot of the elaborate ornamentation was sold off as scrap. The present scrap-merchants seem to be eyeing the machine itself with looks that bode it no good. . . .

To abolish the objectionable trappings of the Treaty and replace it with a constitution rooted in the new state was another pressing matter. The Constitution of 1937 is a much more potent subject for causing apoplexy today than it was at the time. Only sixty-five per cent of the electorate voted in the state's first referendum, and in the General Election held on the same day. Fifty-seven per cent of those who voted approved of the Constitution; only forty-five point three per cent of them voted for Fianna Fáil who failed again to get an overall majority.

Most of the opposition to the document was on the grounds that it would take the state out of the Commonwealth and retard the chances of national reunification (Fine Gael); that it did not establish a Republic (Labour and Republicans without the walls); that it placed the women of Ireland firmly in the kitchen and the labour wards (the small voice of the emancipated women of 1937); that Article 44 did not go far enough in stating the desirable and true position of the Holy Roman Catholic Church ("Maria Duce" and other fringe organisations once comfortably dubbed "lunatic" by self-satisfied liberals); that Articles 2 and 3 were a threat to the territory and people of Northern Ireland (Loyalists, who always meant Loyalists when they used the term "people" in this, and almost every other, context).

It was not a formidable lobby and many of those who voted against the Constitution were merely registering their disapproval of the Economic War and other party political matters. The Fine Gael objection seemed premature and peevish, particularly when the British Government announced that the new Constitution did not affect Irish membership of the Commonwealth. Once again de Valera was having his constitutional cake and eating part of it, at least.

It was noticed that the word "Republic" (or "Poblacht") did not appear in the new document. It was being kept for the day when Ireland was really united and free it seemed. It was also noted that Irish was to be the first official language of the state of Eire: a word still used by sections of the British Press to describe Irish boxers and golfers in defeat who in victory are British. What was not understood was that this remarkable feat of linguistic reversal was to be the upper limit of Fianna Fáil's language policy.

The Gaelic League, most of whose senior members lived in the arse pocket of de Valera's dress suit during the annual Oireachtas, was far too tamed to suggest that it might be a help if the Chief could persuade his Cabinet to give good example by learning and using the language. Only the true begrudgers, and the Gaelic Leaguers who were locked up in jail, were ill-mannered enough to point out that de Valera never said anything of importance in Irish himself, that he merely meandered on about the importance of Irish and that if he was ever rejected at the polls he would go from church gate to church gate exhorting people to love the language. Why he should choose to do that when he had no political power was not clear. Not that it mattered, for when the people did reject him at the polls he immediately set about getting power back again as quickly as possible.

As for the special position of the Catholic Church in the original version of the Constitution, it seems to have been a compromise between what some churchmen wanted and what de Valera was willing to give. In later life he said that Article 44 troubled him more than any other at the time of drafting. There is a bit of "church gatery" about that but it is true that it did not seem to worry the Protestants of the state at the time. The *Irish Times* announced that, "The new Constitution is largely bunkum, and to that extent it is harmless." The *Church of Ireland Gazette* wrote, "The whole thing will not make us any freer, will not indeed make the slightest difference to our affairs."

In 1972, when a referendum was held to delete the reference to the special position of the Catholic Church — in what was to be Jack Lynch's major contribution to the cause of Irish unity — its deletion by a majority of six to one scarcely caused a banner to flutter. The Northern Loyalists said that what happened in a foreign state was of no interest to them; had it been retained by the same margin they would have shouted "Rome Rule". Cardinal Conway said that he would shed no tears over its passing. So what did it all prove?

One thing it did prove is that squeezing blackheads out of the face of the 1937 Constitution to make an impression on Loyalists is a form of constitutional masturbation that does lead to blindness. What we need is a referendum to find out if a majority gives a "monkey's" about re-unification at all, and what manner of national obscurantism is not for bargaining under any circumstances.

As far as the Catholic Church is concerned it is no longer necessary to have the state embroider "We are the Greatest" on its vestments. When you have floored all contenders so many times that the public no longer comes to see the contests it would be a bit of an embarrassment. In these days of sophisticated public relations it is the hidden power that counts. Instead of talking about sin and bigamy you talk about dividing the little bit of land and cutting off the first family with the clippings of tin cans and a technical school education, God help us!

It is as plain as a pikestaff that the Constitution of 1937 is no longer suitable for the present twenty-six-county state with its large Catholic majority. It is just as clear that the chances of changing it in any substantial way are very remote. In the unlikely event of any Irish politician being involved in the drafting of a new constitution for the whole island of Ireland, he would find himself subjected to pressures so extreme that de Valera's lot in 1937 would seem like a bed of roses.

While much of the de Valera bashing that has been

going on for years now, on the head of his Constitution, is merely a substitute for original thought, or the will to implement it if it existed, he has to be faulted severely on one major count.

He handed the Catholic Church the real power it wanted in the areas where real power lay, at a time when he was still negotiating with the British Government on the question of Irish unity. The Catholic Church is as greedy for power as it is experienced in obtaining it when it can. In 1937 it did not have to work very hard to gain control of the areas which it regarded as being of supreme importance: education, the family, health, social matters and the primacy of private property. It has to work a lot harder today to retain that power but seems more than equal to the task.

The only possible explanation for de Valera's lack of any consideration for the Protestants in the northern state is that he was still toying with his notion of transferring the ones that did not measure up to his definition of "Irishness" to Britain — with British co-operation and assistance. Their place would be taken by a like number of British citizens of Irish descent, presumably Catholics,

If this idea sounds crazy to you now it is as well to remind you that Ernest Blythe, in one of his autobiographical works, explains that he only ruled out the short, sharp successful invasion of the Six Counties from the south, as a solution to Partition, because he did not believe our army capable of carrying out the operation. In the 1950s an organisation called "Aiséirí", which had an unhealthy respect for Dr Salazar's Portugal (as if we didn't have it in our own house!), periodically plastered Dublin with posters announcing: "Six Divisions, Six Counties, Six Minutes". Peadar ·Cowan, a Clann na Poblachta and Independent TD and ex-army officer, raised a private army to free the Six Counties by putting advertisements in the newspapers. And finally, a Fianna Fáil backbencher and true begrudger suggested that a south-westerly wind and poison gas was the only real and final solution to the problem of the lost green field. It was to be understood that unlike God poison gas was not capable of recognising "its own" and that a clean sweep was intended.

The backbencher, who was only half joking, was rebuked majestically by de Valera whose own solution seemed to be that the Loyalists either joined us on our terms or got to hell out of our territory. That could be described as having no basic understanding of the problem at all, as his famous reply to Churchill in 1945 clearly showed.

But his greatest offence was not a lack of understanding, which he shared with almost all the politicians of his day who took any interest in the problem, but that he pretended to have a solution to that which he did not understand. For the rest of his political life he kept on referring to the great wrong which was inflicted on our sainted isle and how he was going to set it right with serried ranks of frozen words known as "The Anti-Partition Campaign". To have hanged, shot and interned people who used other means to achieve what he maintained was part of the Holy Trinity of Irish political objectives — while doing nothing practical to deal with it, apart from the words and the pamphlets that only the true believers paid any attention to — was merely to compound one of his cardinal sins as a politician.

The Protestants in the southern state were beginning to trust him, however. He behaved abominably in the affair of the Protestant librarian, Letitia Dunbar-Harrison, prevented by Mayo County Council in 1931 from taking up her appointment as County Librarian, on the spurious grounds that she did not have the required standard of Irish. The same excuse, which did little for the standing of the language in the community, was later used elsewhere to appoint a leading Knight of Columbanus to the position of County Education Officer in preference to a better-qualified non-practicing Catholic who was living apart from his wife.

The Minister for Local Government in the Cumann na nGael Cabinet, Dick Mulcahy, behaved impeccably in the affair. As he usually emerges from the pages of Irish history with all his seventy-seven wounds gaping it is nice to be able to confuse the issue by stating that he comes out of this affair with a veritable stigmata. He even dissolved Mayo County Council for failing to do its duty properly and appointed a commissioner in its place. That battle he won but he lost the war. Poor Miss Letitia Dunbar-Harrison, who must have been specially named to put the fear of Luther into the *Páidíní* West of the Shannon, had to be given a post of far less sensitivity in Dublin.

When speaking in the Dáil on the matter de Valera, who was then in opposition, made an interesting observation: "I say that if I had a vote on a local body, and there were two qualified people who had to deal with a Catholic community, and if one was a Catholic and another a Protestant, I would unhesitatingly vote for the Catholic."

If this was bad news for Protestants who only handled books it was a hundred times worse for Protestant doctors who would be handling, God bless the mark, areas of much greater sensitivity among the deserving poor in the windy dispensaries of rural Ireland. It has been said in de Valera's defence that he was merely telegraphing his post-Civil War orthodoxy to the Catholic Hierarchy. He may also have been bidding for the *Páidín* vote and signalling his approval of Catholic censorship for a mainly Catholic people. What excuses the Labour Party had for taking a similar attitude is still not clear, but it could just have been another example of their *Leanna Mo Chroí's Dog* syndrome: having to go a bit on the road with every Tom, Dick and Harry... but not with a lassie called Letitia mark you!

By 1937 de Valera had impressed the Protestants as the one politician who would stand up to episcopal pressure. This was largely due to his attitude to the Republican Government in Spain, which he continued to recognise, quite properly, as the lawful Government of the country when the Catholic Hierarchy wanted him to give the nod to the Catholic General Franco who wanted to establish a dictatorship, and did.

The *Irish Times* was obliged to withdraw its correspondent who was reporting on the Civil War in Spain when the Catholic Colleges, which for reasons of well-heeled snobbery advertised in the paper, threatened to withdraw their advertising. The final score in that contest was: Pound 1 — Principle 0.

With the passage of time the Protestant Churches found that they could get almost anything they wanted from de Valera by the personal approach, considerable circumspection and by refraining from asking for anything in writing and by knowing their proper place. The training in humility had been successful. It was accepted without question that the token civil servant, army officer, or tame TD (when one could be found) would turn up to represent the Taoiseach or one of his ministers, instead of the organ grinders who turned up for the Catholic ceremonies. In this respect, if in no other, Erskine Childers was the Protestant God's gift to Fianna Fáil.

But even the usually humourless Protestant Bishops, who never seemed to produce a Dr O'Doherty, O'Callaghan, Lucey, Browne or O'Boyle for national edification, must have been amused when de Valera could not attend the church service which preceded the inauguration of the first President of Ireland, Douglas Hyde. Disgruntled Republicans may even have allowed themselves a chuckle or two at the thought of Dev sitting in his office meditating on the other Reserved Sins of the day (sins of such a serious nature that only a bishop could cleanse them from the soul): membership of an illegal organisation, poitín-making and perjury.

At least he had the gumption not to sit outside the Cathedral in his car as John A. Costello and his Cabinet did on the occasion of Dr Hyde's funeral. However, that piece of nonsense inspired Austin Clarke to write a poem.

De Valera, apart from his remarkable appearance in *Finnegans Wake*, was not a great source of creativity in others. He inspired very few jokes and his own attempts at humour were so mathematical and predictable that they fell as flat as flounders on a wet deck. The new Constitution produced one mildly funny story, probably of the "Cosgrave and the Pope" school of creativity, but nevertheless worth recording.

When de Valera went through the final version of the new Constitution with his cabinet, one minister remarked that Dónal Ó Buachalla was going to be out of a job.

De Valera, who had been playing his cards very close to his chest, decided that it was time he took his friend, who had served his country as an "Old Armpit" in the bad days, into his confidence and rang him up there and then.

After exchanging meaningless Gaelic League type pleasantries about "an aimsir" and "an chúis" de Valera got down to business, as was his wont, in what was soon going to become the second official language.

"A Dhónaill, I have to tell you that you're abolished."

There was a puzzled and shocked silence at the other end of the line and then came the angry rejoinder.

"And I'd like to tell you, a Eamoinn, that you're another!"

The negotiations with the British Prime Minister, Neville Chamberlain, which were concluded in April 1938, were the crowning achievement of the new Taoiseach's dealings with Britain. As well as getting rid of the objectionable trappings of the Treaty it got rid of the two more important issues of substance: the ports and the annuities. De Valera retained his curious relationship with the Crown on a long and almost invisible halter but on the matter of the lost green field he came up against the usual stone wall. But he was happy that the Economic War was over and that Chamberlain, in an excess of appeasement, handed him the means to declare the country neutral in the war that was about to envelop Europe and the world.

This time it was scarcely necessary to look into his heart before calling a general election for June in which he won a thumping fifty-two per cent of the votes cast and an over-all majority of seats. Much to his delight Labour had chosen the moment of his greatest popularity to vote with Fine Gael and bring down the Government. De Valera would probably have found an excuse for an early election anyway but it was great to have been saved the trouble.

8

"If you had a dog would you treat it in that fashion?"

As soon as the Dáil had declared for neutrality the Government re-defined the state the rest of the world had got itself into: calling it an "Emergency" instead of a "War". This decision has always given rise to a certain amount of derision but it was just another Irish solution to an Irish problem: we were not at war yet nobody could deny that we were also living in abnormal times. We began to turn in on ourselves.

When the playwright Denis Johnston returned to Dublin, during a break from his duties as a war correspondent with the BBC, and attempted to give a first-hand account of the hostilities to his cronies in the Pearl Bar, he was immediately put in his place by Patrick Kavanagh. The poet told him bluntly that he found the war very boring. And in a leading article in the *Bell* magazine the editor, Seán O'Faoláin, described how he had to sit impatiently through a long report on that day's pilgrimage to Croagh Patrick and various other items of home news before Radio Eireann chose to give the latest details of the war in Europe. It was that kind of Emergency all right.

There was no doubt but that the vast majority of the population regarded neutrality as the right policy. It was only partly a protest against partition. It was the first opportunity to assert our independence and a small blow for the freedom of small nations to stay out of big power conflicts; not that this principle did Belgium, Holland,

Norway and Denmark a lot of good when Hitler chose to breach their frontiers.

What really saved Ireland from being occupied by either American or British forces as a "protective measure" — as happened to Iceland after the German invasion of Denmark — was the availability of the ports and airfields of Northern Ireland, although it was not considered patriotic to draw attention to that at the time.

Those who wanted to join the British forces were perfectly free to do so and about 50,000 did, some deserting from the Irish army after training, thereby being assured of rapid promotion. One conspicuous absentee from this flight of the wild geese was a man who was later to lead the Fine Gael party.

James Dillon was the only member of the Dáil to vote in favour of entering the war on the Allied side. But having been expelled from Fine Gael for his good intentions he seemed to mislay them somewhere for he spent the war years — he surely would have refused to accept the term Emergency — running his business in Ballaghadereen (curiously christened Monica Duff's) and earning himself a page in the annals of Irish begrudgery.

Principles apart, we had little to gain from becoming involved in the war. We would probably have lost as many citizens to German bombs as we did to emigration and Dublin would have been flattened and rebuilt more or less as it now is. One of the few possible benefits might have been some good harbours along the west and south coasts — Blacksod, Galway and Fenit, for instance — which might in time have been developed for the benefit of a real fishing industry. However, they could also have been left to moulder away like the little Famine piers one sees in the oddest places along the coast.

On the other hand the Bog of Allen would by now have swallowed Tullamore as well as many smaller towns in the midlands. For the real benefit of the Emergency was that we were forced to stand on our own feet for six years and face the harsher realities of independence and attempted self-sufficiency. The real tragedy was that the lessons were not even half-learned and the country still remains an under-developed mess, albeit with ideas above its station.

But to make neutrality possible we had to give the impression, at least, of being ready and able to defend the state against all comers. A great recruiting drive was launched and, as you will read in all the best books on the period, old Civil War enemies sat on the same platforms and asked people to join the same National Army. This is meant to make you feel rightly good and warm inside and just a little emotional. It is a feeling guaranteed to be free from any subversive contamination.

There is no doubt but that the regular force of 15,000, with a reserve of about 12,000 — and God only knows how many willing members of the Local Security Force and the Local Defence Force, later to become the FCA, or Free Clothing Association — would have taken on all comers. The spirit of real warfare was still alive in the land. Kilmichael and Crossbarry had not yet been given the "Let O'Brien Shift It" treatment. Ill-equipped as they were, these men would have done their almighty best.

What tends to chill the warm feeling and melt the lump in the throat rather quickly is the fact that twenty-five years later a much better equipped army of 14,000 (many with experience abroad with the UNO peace-keeping force) and a reserve of 17,000, was considered unfit to intervene in Northern Ireland to protect part of the national majority and to make the partition of Ireland the international issue all governments claimed they wished to make it. We were told that our army would be put to the pin of its collar to hold South Armagh: something a bunch of Provos have since come as near as makes no difference to doing without benefit of square-bashing or getting warring tribes to kiss and make up.

Instead of putting up or shutting up, the Government of the day was reduced to buying guns from a knacker in Hamburg which they then failed to smuggle into the state they were supposed to rule because the Special Branch stopped them. The army was used to protect the Border the Government said it wanted abolished and continued to keep the peace as far from home as foreign wars allowed.

All in all these events took away from the spirit of the men who would have taken on the German paratroopers in 1940. As Myles na Gopaleen once wrote, "Do spile sé an effect."

Apart from James Dillon there were not many begrudgers around during the Emergency and those who were took care to keep their voices down. Some West Britons made jokes about shop-boys joining the army in the hopes of becoming generals like their mothers before them. This was not even original. Tim Healy had said it years previously about the IRA while compiling his national record. There were stories about recruits insisting that they wanted to join the navy because they liked the thought of being able to cycle to home to their dinners every day.

But most stories concerned the various forms of deprivation that afflicted people as all imported goods disappeared from the shelves under the counters. Smokers were hit hardest of all. It was not unusual to see as many as half a dozen people sharing a cigarette in a hayfield after drinking their weak tea.

A farmer near the Border, who had been out of tobacco for days, was shocked to see his neighbour smoking his pipe energetically while ploughing the field next to him. This display of greed and selfishness annoyed him and made his teeth water. But when he was met at the headland by a now pipeless neighbour he immediately replied in the negative when asked if he had ever tried smoking dried cow-dung.

"I'll tell you something for nothing now," said his neighbour, "You've missed sweet fuck all."

The big cattle producers, just recovering from the slaughter of innocent calves during the Economic War, looked forward to making a fortune out of the war as their ancestors had done during previous conflicts. A terrible outbreak of foot-and-mouth disease hit the country and their stocks were slaughtered all over again. To compound their misery the Government forced them to grow wheat so that people would have some bread to eat. But so patriotic were these beneficiaries of the Land League that compulsory tillage orders had to be invoked, and some who disobeyed them had to be threatened with even harsher penalties if they did not do their duty. In any serious situation in Ireland compulsion is either a first or last resort.

It has been noted by most observers of the Irish scene, during this period and even later, that the country was the greatest example of state ownership in Europe outside of the Soviet Union. Apart from the land, almost everything of value and importance was run by the state — which was passing strange in a country where "socialism" was just as dirty a word as "communism". The secret was in not using that dirty word at all: at not even hinting that running railways at one remove, through a board nominated by the state, was a form of the dreaded menace that always ended in the rape of nuns and the turning of churches into palaces of culture.

The most spectacular of the many semi-state bodies established at this time was Irish Shipping, although Bord na Móna was equally important as well as proving more durable. Frank Aiken, always de Valera's right-hand man more than Seán Lemass, went to the USA to buy what ships he could lay a cheque-book on. These ships kept the country supplied with essential commodities while the war lasted and lives were lost when combatants, by design or accident, sank some of them.

James Dillon did not raise many laughs when he said that some of these ships, purchased on the west coast of America, were in such bad condition that the authorities were reluctant to let them through the Panama Canal in case they sank and blocked it. It was a bad time for begrudgers as we have said. But the eventual sale of what was left of the once-proud fleet, in 1985, did not raise many laughs either; nor did it lead to the political row one would have expected in an under-developed country.

The country survived but it also stagnated. There is a myth abroad that Ireland was the happiest patch in the world between 1939 and 1945. It is associated in a strange way with de Valera's ideal of villages ringing with the laughter of comely maidens and the patter of little legitimate feet. Many of the comely maidens were earning good money in England, taking their chances with Hitler's bombs and a pagan society, and many of the little children suffered from the effects of an unbalanced diet.

Tuberculosis stalked the land and in spite of threats and penalties some shopkeepers short-rationed their less well-heeled customers and sold tea and other scarce goods at great profit on the black market.

But the country survived and it was a lot better than being a cock-shot for Hitler's air force. A lot of excitement was generated by rumours of invasion. Apart from their sending over some of the most inept spies in the history of espionage, the Germans were not really a threat once Hitler succeeded in kicking a reluctant Soviet Union into its anti-Nazi crusade in June 1941 by invading it. Information available after the war showed that the American threat was more serious than it appeared to be in 1944 when they called for the expulsion of the German and Japanese ambassadors. The British played matters in a lower key once they realised that Ireland was really neutral on their side and de Valera played his role on the diplomatic front with a perfection that puts him in a different class to his immediate successors, not to mention the present-day lot of butter-fingered pass-droppers.

De Valera gave the impression, as he always did, that in spite of his oft-repeated dedication to Caitlín Ní Uallacháin's thorny way, he was at his best and happiest when allowed to dance one of his intricate jigs on a corner of the world stage. Having to remain spancelled inside three green fields, and only able to peer over the wall into the fourth one, did not suit his style at all. The island's parochial problems certainly dragged him down to their level and he seemed to lack the particular will to rise above them and kick them into shape. He talked better policies than most of the Taoisigh who followed him, with the exception of a couple who found it difficult to articulate at all, and that was about the height of it.

Twice during the Emergency de Valera tried to turn the country's claustrophobic patriotism to Fianna Fáil's advantage at the polls. In the General Election of 1943, instead of being returned in triumph as the protector of his people, he actually lost his over-all majority.

Labour benefitted from urban dissatisfaction with food shortages, wet turf, low wages and unemployment. Rural dissatisfaction with almost everything under the sun found an outlet in a new political party, Clann na Talún. It was founded in 1938 to deal with the grievances of the not too horny-handed Children of the Soil and enjoyed a brief period of success, in the 40s and 50s, in parts of the west and south. Its last surviving TD, Michael Donnellan, died in Croke Park as his son John was captaining Galway to success in the All-Ireland football final. John joined Fine Gael and won and held the seat. Fianna Fáil believed that John was open to negotiations but the fixer who was sent to make the political match delayed to talk to men about some dogs and, according to party folklore, found Gerry Sweetman's car parked outside the homestead.

Clann na Talún was unique among Irish political parties to gain representation in Dáil Eireann by having almost no policies apart from remedying farmers' griev-ances: a task beyond human, or even divine, competence. The party once held seventeen seats, a little-known fact that tells us more than could be good for our peace of mind about Irish politics. However, the party did contain many colourful characters and made its contribution to political folklore if not to political thought.

Fianna Fáil formed a Government with the assistance of some independents but, as always in such circumstances, de Valera was uneasy and already looking with increasing disfavour at Proportional Representation. In May 1944, a minor provision of the Transport Bill (more nationalisation) was defeated when two Independent deputies voted against the Government. Their names were Cole and Byrne and they fuelled many a joke in the pages of *Dublin Opinion*. De Valera had a quick look into his heart before driving up to Áras an Uachtaráin in the middle of the night to dissolve the Dáil; he almost precipitated a Presidential Election such was the shock to Douglas Hyde's ageing nervous system.

This time the magic worked. Aided in no small way by the American Note he won another over-all majority.

The War ended but the Emergency lingered on and it looked as if Fianna Fáil was going to be in power for another decade at least: a depressing thought which was not going to do the party a bit of good eventually. Winston Churchill did de Valera a good turn by attacking Ireland's neutrality intemperately and enabling the Taoiseach to give his most outstanding display of virtuosity in a radio broadcast after which even IRA-men and Blueshirts became misty-eyed for brief moments.

During the war Churchill had sent him an emotional telegram which seemed to offer Irish re-unification in return for the use of our ports. De Valera wisely refused to rise to the false bait but in his reply to Churchill's attack he likened the partition of Ireland to the occupation of six English counties by a foreign power. So, Brits out was the solution to our problem? But it was not a time for raising eyebrows: some of those who later did were too busy planning an anti-partition campaign which was going to work the miracle anyway. In the circumstances "Up Dev" was all that needed to be said.

The first sign that Fianna Fáil's position was not as un-assailable as it seemed came when the people voted in a presidential election for the first time in 1945. Seán T. O Ceallaigh had an easy enough win over Fine Gael's Seán MacEoin but a third candidate, an Independent Republican called Patrick MacCartan, polled 200,000 votes, many of them in Dublin.

The following year a group who had come together in

Dublin to assist Republican prisoners founded a new party, Clann na Poblachta, under the leadership of Seán MacBride. As Irish had become the first official language of the state the new party was generally known as "The Klan". It deserves a much closer look from historians than either its life-span or numerical strength in the Dáil would seem to warrant. It was — and still remains — the first sign that the post-Civil War, two-and-a-half party system could be broken. Some observers, in the ranks of Old Believer-Republicans and in Fianna Fáil itself, noticed that it bore an uncanny resemblance to Fianna Fáil in 1932. However, it was the difference between it and the Party of Reality that wrecked it before it managed to sail into clear water.

Fianna Fáil found that whatever form of patriotism sustained its followers for fourteen years was now turning rapidly into post-war weariness and disillusionment. The ministers who looked so energetically raw in 1932 now seemed elderly and sapped of energy and ideas. De Valera was to find out, as other leaders before and after him found out, that there comes a moment when even a defeated IRA becomes a force to be reckoned with. The repressive measures he found so obnoxious when applied to the IRA by Free State and Cumann na nGael Governments now had him by the throat.

When Seán MacCaughey died in Portlaoise Prison in May 1946, after a hunger and thirst strike, many people had forgotten the details of the sordid Stephen Hayes affair for which MacCaughey had been sentenced to death and reprieved. It was the report of the inquest, held in prison, that shocked the country. Seán MacBride, who appeared for the next-of-kin, was not allowed to cross-examine the prison governor but he asked the medical officer some damaging questions.

Mr MacBride: Are you aware that during the four and half years he was here he was never out in the fresh air or sunlight?

Dr Duane: As far as I am aware he was not.

Mr MacBride: Would I be right in saying that up to twelve or thirteen months ago he was kept in solitary confinement and not allowed to speak or associate with any other person?

Dr Duane: That is right.

Mr MacBride: Would you treat a dog in that fashion?

Mr McLoughlin (for the authorities): That is not a proper question.

Mr MacBride: If you had a dog would you treat it in that fashion?

Dr Duane: (after a pause) No.

Apart from the prisoners who were "on the blanket" in Portlaoise there was trouble threatening Fianna Fáil on other fronts. The teachers' strike, mentioned earlier, only affected the Dublin national teachers directly but every teacher in the country was levied for the strike fund. The Minister for Education, Tomás O Deirig, a rather weak person at the best of times (when Dr Dinneen, the lexicographer, heard of his appointment to the Department he commented: "Tá an t-oideachas ag dul chun deirig anois") was not allowed to negotiate by de Valera, And not alone did he snub the Archbishop of Dublin's effort to make peace but he slapped down his old comrade, Seán Moylan, when he intervened. Teachers deserted Fianna Fáil in numbers and many of them threw in their lot with Clann na Poblachta.

But as well as these obvious cases of concern, the revulsion against the grey claustrophobic aspect of the country, the stagnant economy and the new surge of emigration as America "opened up" again, there was a feeling that Dev and his party had been in charge for too long and that the country could do with a change of political air and scenery.

The 1948 election was the first of the "Put Them Out" contests and although Fianna Fáil recovered from the shock of finding itself in opposition, the country saw that life did not end under Coalition Governments. Most elections since 1948 have been of the "Put Them Out" variety, and the next one looks like being no exception. One definite exception was the General Election of 1977, when Jack Lynch, Martin O'Donoghue, George Colley and Séamus Brennan offered such good value for peoples' votes that only the blind and the very saintly could refuse.

But Fianna Fáil received the final push down the slipway from a series of scandals, and rumours of scandals, that always seem to attach to Governments too long in power and too practised in patronage. An over-cautious press, a trussed radio station and a public eager for forms of excitement other than that which the GAA provided, made word of mouth even more important than it is today; and even today only a fool would underestimate its importance.

Two of the scandals were very minor ones. One concerned a bacon factory in Monaghan in which Dr Con Ward, a Parliamentary Secretary in the Fianna Fáil Government, was involved. A tribunal of enquiry cleared Dr Ward of all the allegations made by a disgruntled ex-employee apart from a minor sin of omission in an income tax return. De Valera requested his resignation, which was a severe blow to the party as Dr Ward was nego-tiating important health legislation at the time. This was an early example of the high standards required by Fianna Fáil from its members and ministers, which established a tradition that flourished with the passage of time to the consternation of its enemies.

The other minor scandal concerned alleged irregu-larities on the stock exchange by a friend of Seán Lemass, which was really another attempt by Fine Gael to scupper Lemass himself. It was devious and malicious, but not really as puke-making as the party's present attempts to portray Lemass (not to mention de Valera and Jack Lynch) as latter-day saints who were loved and trusted by

111

the party that would never dream of stooping low to conquer.

The third scandal was the one that really did for Fianna Fáil. It concerned a distillery, a group of foreigners with exotic names, gold watches as bribes for the highest in the land, the London black market, a man who was not who he seemed to be and who disappeared off the deck of the mail-boat at night and the ringmaster who made this outlandish cast answer to the cracking of his whip, Oliver J. Flanagan, then the youngest TD in Dáil Eireann in the interests of the Monetary Reform party, Laois-Offaly, and the Creator of all things.

Starting smears and rumours was easier then than now and, as the saying goes, "they were all at it". For instance, a Clann na Talún TD in the west of Ireland, about this time, announced to a startled audience one Sunday that they were only hearing "the half of what was going on". Up in Dublin, he continued, it was common knowledge that de Valera himself was up to his ears in a sleazy cosmetics factory run by some central European Communists. This was particularly galling for Fianna Fáil who had almost patented the "Communist" smear in a successful campaign to split the Labour Party.

However, this was a new one on them and the rumour had grown a million legs before it was realised that the Child of the Soil was referring to the Dublin School of Cosmic Physics which de Valera had helped to found and in which a Hungarian refugee, a scholar of renown, was employed.

But for the national and supernatural record of Oliver Flanagan the Monetary Reform party would have long since fallen through the footnotes of history into oblivion. It was part of a small European movement of a quasi-Catholic bent which had a certain popularity in France. How it put down a tender root in Laois is not clear. A recent magazine article on Oliver Flanagan found one speech from an early member who said the party was going to put the land of Ireland at the disposal of the young people of Ireland and blamed governments for the instability of the money market. He seemed to advocate a simple solution to this: to put more money into circulation. But things were a little more complicated than that for, "it is the financial Scrooges who control the rise, the Jews and the Freemasons who have its control and who hold the country in their grasp."

Stirring stuff in its own way but not a patch on what was happening down the road in Kilbeggan where Locke's Distillery was in the process of being bought by a parcel of international crooks, aided and abetted by a large section of the Fianna Fáil party and assorted hangers-on. There was a Georges Eindiguer (who even in 1947 had a private plane), a Herr Saschell (who had acquired a farm of land in Galway, nudge-wink-nudge) and the Daddy of them all, Horace Henry Smith, who was not really Horace Henry Smith at all but a registered crook called Alexander Maximoe.

He seems to have been the only casualty of the affair, if he did what he was supposed to have done. For he was deported and put aboard the mailboat at Dún Laoire but never arrived at the other side of the Irish Sea. People heard a splash and saw a figure disappear but no body was ever found. Some said he was the last artist forced to leave Ireland. But in Dublin folklore he lived on, for it was believed that he reappeared as Dr Paul Singer, the stamp swindler, years later when the heat was off.

This was Ireland's first international-style scandal and helped more than anything else to break Fianna Fáil's morale and led to the party's downfall, the country's first Coalition Government (although it was rather quaintly known as Inter-Party), the establishment of the Irish Republic and Dr Noel Browne's Mother and Child Scheme out of which modern political history grew, as you of the post-referenda period know so well.

Alas, so much is forgotten. Poor Maximoe, if he did really dive to his death, is now remembered only by the

occasional begrudger longing for the days of political
simplicity, in a little rhyme:

> Eeeny, meeny Maximoe,
> Catch James Dillon by the toe,
> If he screams 'Oliver' let him go,
> Eeeny, meeny Maximoe.

9

De Valera, the gold watch and 60,000 gallons of whiskey

The central facts of the Locke's Distillery furore are very simple. After the war there was a great shortage of mature whiskey on the European and British markets. An outfit called Trans-World Trust of Lausanne showed an interest in buying the Kilbeggan distillery when it came on the market in 1947. The big attraction was the 60,000 gallons of whiskey in stock, worth about £660,000 on the London black market.

Eindiguer and Horace Henry Smith contacted a Clonmel solicitor with a view to buying the distillery and he put them in touch with a firm of auctioneers who would handle the sale. A prominent Fianna Fáil Senator was a partner in the firm. The sale seemed to be progressing smoothly to the point when a deposit was demanded. When it was not paid within the time allowed the contract of sale was repudiated. It was at that point that suspicions were awakened about the foreign parties and their various associates and the police and Department of Justice officials were alerted. At the time there were a lot of shady men around, in search of shady deals which they hoped to clinch with the aid of shady money. In this case it seems the money, shady or otherwise, did not materialise in time.

Eindiguer was found without much difficulty in a Dún Laoire hotel. His Swiss passport was in order but he left the country the following day never to return. Horace Henry Smith, Eindiguer's interpreter and general dogsbody, was more difficult to locate as he was on the run from the authorities. When located it was discovered that he was really Alexander Maximoe, travelling on a British passport falsely obtained, and wanted by the British police on a criminal charge. He was deported to places unknown. Another associate, Herr Saschell, was living on a farm he owned near Gort and displaying an unhealthy interest in tweed. After being warned about doing business in Ireland he was also requested to leave the country, which he did.

While all this was going on the matter was raised in the Dáil by Oliver Flanagan, who was doing his own detective work with the intention of exposing what he believed to be a Fianna Fáil plot to sell part of the national assets to foreign con-men and their con-ladies. He was given some assistance, until the going got tough, by Dominic Cafferky of Clann na Talún, with interesting interventions from James Dillon and Paddy McGilligan. Various Government Ministers, TDs and assorted hangers-on were accused of having had slugs out of the whiskey bottles.

Oliver Flanagan, then in his prime as a witch-hunter, made full use of the Dáil's facilities by "smearing" right, left and centre and becoming a national figure in the process. Among the most colourful allegations was one concerning gold watches Herr Eindiguer was advised to present to the Taoiseach and his son, by the Fianna Fáil Senator, as a small token of his esteem. Suddenly, everyone in the country was talking about Dev's gold watch.

After much heat had been generated and much dirt thrown at people, inside and outside the Dáil, the Government announced that a Judicial Tribunal was being set up to examine all the allegations. When Deputy Dillon asked that there should be cross-examination of witnesses, Seán Lemass, who had taken a lot of stick during the affair to date, snorted, "Yes, and imprisonment for anyone who perjures himself."

The Tribunal was composed of three Judges, Cahir Davitt, John O'Byrne and Kevin Haugh. Its hearing filled many columns in the daily papers as Deputy Flanagan repeated his revelations about Fianna Fáil and the international three-card-tricksters. But the other Deputies who had come in on his slipstream in the Dáil were conspicuous by their absence from the Tribunal. Gallant Oliver's only witnesses were Joseph Cooney (Senior), Secretary of Locke's Distillery, and his son, Joseph Cooney (Junior). When his own evidence and theirs seemed to meet head-on, Deputy Flanagan requested that Eindiguer, Saschell and two women named Chapelle and Dunnico be found and summoned before the Tribunal.

The Tribunal refused, saying that, in their view, the application was frivolously made. It seemed at this stage that God had deserted Oliver Flanagan in his hour of need: a feeling reinforced by the Tribunal's findings which were made public in December 1947.

Naturally, human nature being what it is, most readers homed in on the gold watch and must have been disappointed to find the Tribunal most dismissive:

"In our opinion there is no foundation for this allegation and we consider that the charge contained in it was made with extravagant recklessness and complete absence of a sense of responsibility."

Great prominence was given in the newspapers to the Tribunal's assessment of Deputy Flanagan's own evidence:

... We found it necessary to exercise extreme caution in dealing with the evidence of Deputy Flanagan. We found him very uncandid and much disposed to answer questions unthinkingly and as if he were directing his replies elsewhere than to the Tribunal. On several occasions he contradicted himself and was disposed to shift his ground, when he found that answers already given would lead him where he did not wish to go. He was, on other occasions, in conflict with testimony which we believed to be true. In respect of two matters we are satisfied that he told us what he knew to be untrue. One of these was of little importance save as a test of his credibility. The other was of some importance.

He denied that he took any notes of his first interview with Mr Cooney, Junior. Mr Cooney said he did and was not cross-examined upon this. Recalled specially upon this point towards the close of our sittings, Mr Cooney repeated this evidence and again was not cross-examined. We are satisfied, and so find, that Deputy Flanagan did take notes at this interview and we can attribute his denial only to the supposition that the notes, if produced, would not substantiate his evidence as to what Mr Cooney told him. In the circumstances, in so far as the matter is material, we feel more disposed to accept Mr Cooney's evidence relating to that interview than that of Deputy Flanagan.

All that was bad enough, but the Tribunal also found that there was no foundation for the allegations made against prominent people. It looked as if Fianna Fáil had rid themselves of the Laois-Offaly thorn in the party's side. But the result of the General Election in February showed that the people of Laois-Offaly could read the smoke signals even if they could not see the flames or feel the heat of the fire. Oliver Flanagan topped the poll, increasing his vote by almost 5,000 to 14,370; more than the great poll-topper Seán Lemass got in Dublin, or Eamon de Valera himself got in Clare. God is not mocked, after all.

Most commentators now agree that it was de Valera's decision to call an early election after Clann na Poblachta won two out of three bye-elections, in October 1947, that forced the scarcely half-organised party into many of the errors that hastened its demise. Although it won ten seats, it lost at least as many more by very small margins and instead of maximising its vote, the tactic of having two candidates in each constituency actually did damage in a lot of instances. But it did win six of those ten seats in Dublin and it can still be argued that if Seán MacBride had played his cards differently after the election, by using his party outside the coalition, Clann na Poblachta could have survived and the course of Irish politics changed dramatically.

But the pressure for a change was great, although Seán MacBride barely managed to persuade his Ard-Chomhairle to vote for participation. Fianna Fáil was still the biggest party in the Dáil and Fine Gael had polled the lowest vote in its history. Fine Gael needed a taste of power very badly but in a Dáil full of small parties and Independents the grouping that really held the balance of power at the end of the negotiations on a ten point plan of action, was National Labour.

In addition to its many other problems the Labour Movement, such as it was, was now represented by two parties: Labour and National Labour. National Labour was a creation of William O'Brien, Secretary of the Irish Transport and General Workers Union, aided by that great meddler in public and private affairs, Dr Alfred O'Rahilly, then President of University College Cork; aided and abetted by Seán Lemass and Seán MacEntee who launched a particularly vicious "Red" smear in 1943.

The Labour Party, led by that most unlikely extremist William Norton, had just welcomed back into the fold, as members and as election candidates, Jim Larkin, Sr. and his son, Jim. Not alone were the Larkins portrayed as "real, live Commies" but to William O'Brien their arrival meant an end to political life as he wished it to be. National Labour (Catholic and mainly Rural) was founded and James Everett — of literary and settle-bed fame — was appointed leader.

Fianna Fáil set out to kick manners and a sense of place into its illegitimate political child, but as de Valera considered coalitions bad for stability (and for Fianna Fáil) there were no ministries on offer and although the matter was considered to be in doubt up to the day the Dáil met, National Labour participated.

There was a major row about who was to be Taoiseach. Despite their election slogan, "We do not care what shirt you wore", Clann na Poblachta found John A. Costello's shade of blue easier on the eye than Dick Mulcahy's, the Fine Gael Party leader. This snub could be classified as the last recorded death-rattle of the Civil War for the people were just about to witness a remarkable transformation.

There were rows too about who was to get the ministry, the kudos, the car and the eventual pension. Dr Noel Browne, who had taken the third seat in Dublin South East for Clann na Poblachta, on the heels of John A. Costello and Seán MacEntee, was the greatest surprise of all in getting the party's second ministry, Seán MacBride opting for External Affairs. The irony of Dr Browne's appointment to Health is that as an unknown in politics he belonged to no faction and nobody really knew much about him — least of all the party leader as events were to show — apart from his burning ambition to rid the country of the scourge of TB.

As happened in 1932 when Fianna Fáil formed its first Government, the passage of power out of de Valera's hands into those of John A. Costello in 1948 was not at all dramatic, apart from one heartfelt cry from the snipe-grass. "Thank God I have lived to see this day" was the pious ejaculation with which Oliver J. Flanagan marked the occasion. Then the first Coalition, or Inter-Party, Government got down to work for what was to prove a hectic three years.

To the surprise of many and the consternation of all who wished to see old political moulds preserved, the Government came flying out of its corner rearing for a scrap. At long last it looked as if our basic natural resources were going to be developed. As Minister for Agriculture, James Dillon began to talk wonderful policies. Land was to be reclaimed and enriched, forestry was to be developed (a major item in Clann na Poblachta's manifesto), the fishing grounds were to be exploited and harbours constructed and better markets for all our produce procured.

Some were worried by the extravagant language used by Dillon. He was going to "smother Britain in eggs" and he was going to "throw all the rocks in Connemara into the sea". But when an American columnist, Louella Parsons, met him and described him as "the first real Irishman she ever met" everyone relaxed. He was only a stage-Irishman after all and that mattered little if the magic was going to work.

The people of the Gaeltacht felt warmly towards him. If the people of Connemara worried about what they would have left to stand on, when all the rocks were gone, the people of Aran looked forward to a causeway to the mainland. When he showered them all with day-old chicks which were going to produce the eggs to smother Britain he actually added a word to the language still in everyday use. For many years after the benefactor had returned once more to the sanctuary of Monica Duff's, to take the waters, day-old chicks were known in the Gaeltacht as "Dillons bheaga" (Little Dillons).

Then to prove that all ideological divisions between Fianna Fáil and the other parties in Dáil Eireann were ended, the Taoiseach announced that a Republic was going to be declared; the word in the dictionaries as well as the definitions were now going to apply to the twenty-six-county state. De Valera shouted "Beware! What about the Commonwealth?" but had little choice except to accept the change. His hardest fight was with his own "rearguard" who wanted to vote against the measure on the old principle of "Vingince, be Jasus". These he placated by boycotting the ceremonies that marked the proclamation of the Republic — apart from the special masses, of course. In all matters there had to be a sense of proportion.

The IRA, still knocked out but beginning to move its limbs, would soon bring the gun back into politics again in yet another campaign to rescue the fourth green field. In this they were assisted by the Labour Government in Britain who, in response to a plea from the Loyalists, introduced the Ireland Act of 1949. This seemed to give the permanent Loyalist majority in Northern Ireland the cast-iron guarantee of tenure they required to reassure them that the foot and the boot would remain in place forever.

In the newly-declared Republic there was fury on all sides. The legislation which had been introduced to take the gun out of politics — or at least southern politics, for this was MacBride's real motive in pushing for a Republic — had now been thrown back into its teeth and the door double-locked against Irish unity. There were open-air mass meetings and a promise of bigger and better anti-partition campaigns. An Irish News Agency was established to bring "Ireland's message" to the world by jumping over Britain's "paper wall".

At a great hosting of Gaels in O'Connell Street a political leader announced that we would hit Britain "in her pride and in her pocket", a speech which must have raised a smile on the faces of the fellows with the cardboard suitcases as they passed the meeting on their way to catch the boat-train at Westland Row.

Before we come to Noel Browne and the events that really earned a special place in contemporary history for the first Coalition, it is important to understand a little about that peculiar phenomenon known in political and social — and indeed literary — shorthand as the 50s. Some observers maintain that there would have been hardly any 50s had the Coalition not foundered so tragically; others contend that its sinking was what the 50s were all about. But these are minor academic points to fill odd corners of dubious doctorates.

What is now important is to comprehend that the 50s really began in the mid-40s and lasted well into the mid-60s. Some would argue that traces of the 50s may still be detected today. They point to some of the pronouncements made during the Divorce Referendum of 1986: such as the sermon given by one priest in which he declared that another priest, who had said that Catholics could in conscience vote for having civil divorce, should have been suspended "by a rope".

The 50s meant repression, emigration, clerical domination, spurious patriotism and an educational system that seemed to train people to be physically fearless and morally cowardly. Some of these elements have been treated more than once in our narrative; others need to be dealt with by giving some examples of what people were told to do and, more frequently, what not to do.

The matter of Communism and Socialism we have touched on. These largely unknown and mysterious ideologies were the 50s equivalent of AIDS. The scare of this fate worse than death was used by politicians and priests alike to bolster the particular kind of capitalist values the state mirrored; while at the same time they ignored the extent of state intervention in areas where our native gombeen men feared to tread.

Liberated young people who have seen that much-loved gentleman, Michael O'Riordan of the Communist Party of Ireland ("Red" Riordan, whose name rang out from many a sulphurous pulpit in the 50s), putting his case to a television audience, or who have seen Eoin O Murchú gathering a vote for each day of the year for the CPI in a bye-election in Oliver J. Flanagan's constituency, may laugh loud and long at the state of superstition in Ireland in their fathers' time. They would do well to stifle their sniggers and reflect.

Well within the last twenty years Peter Berry, the powerful secretary of the Department of Justice, came tearing into the Minister's office one morning with dreadful news. He had just been informed by the Special Branch that no less a personage than the Chief Justice, Cearbhall O Dálaigh, had attended a meeting of the Irish Soviet Friendship Society the previous night. It is all very well to say that Peter Berry had paranoia like most Irishmen have catarrh, but he also had the power to flatten Jack Lynch during the arms furore with the kind of bureaucratic shoulder his long career in hurling had not prepared him for.

The 50s was also about the sanctity of the family, purity, the dignity of poverty and the dangers of emigration to pagan societies. We have seen how censorship of books and films, the manner in which the educational system was controlled by the church and the ban on contraceptives played their part in creating the ideal society. Social activities such as drinking and dancing were also subject to strict clerical supervision. It was because of the latter restrictions that the Fleadh Cheoil of the early 60s seemed to mark the end of the Dark Ages, when it was really no more than a manifestation of what was considered normal among civilised people.

Let us begin with purity, as that was the ideal all restrictive measures were meant to protect and promote. The following extracts are from a Catholic Truth Society pamphlet of the period entitled "Can I keep pure?", which was on sale in all well-appointed churches and given to secondary school pupils to read during annual retreats.

> Hence, the pleasure of sex is secondary, a means to an end and to make it an end in itself, or deliberately to do this, is a mortal sin. . . . Let a tiger once taste blood and he becomes mad for more. . . . The poor victim is swept off his feet by passion, and decides, for the time being at any rate, that nothing matters except this violent spasm of pleasure. . . . Happier a thousand times is the beggar shivering in his rags at the street corner if his heart be pure, than the millionaire rolling by in his car if he be impure. . . . The boy and girl have to avoid whatever of its very nature is morally certain to excite sexual pleasure. That is why they are warned about late hours; about prolonged signs of their God-given affection which cheapen so easily, about wandering off alone into places where they are morally certain to succumb to temptation. . . . So girls of all sorts, the short and the stocky, the fat and the scraggy, the pigeon-chested and the knock-kneed, insist on exposing their regrettable physical misfortunes to the ironic gaze of the easily-amused world around them. . . . How any mother can allow her small daughter to romp and play with her brothers without knickers on is incomprehensible and quite disgraceful.

Those who did not or could not read had their ears lashed with pastorals. These they could not escape, except by emigrating, for to miss mass except through grievous illness was a sure sign of lunacy, or worse, and called for instant treatment. It was through these pastorals, and the sermons which were based on them, that the Catholic Church moulded the people in the image it had created for Irish society. In theory, at least, this society still exists, in case the point should pass unnoticed.

All aspects of life were covered, from orthodox erection to glorious resurrection, with particular emphasis on the simple pleasures available in rural areas:

> On various excuses permission is sought in courts to prolong dances; indeed, this permission is being sought so often that some people have got the impression that the Diocesan Rule has been relaxed, and that the closing of dance halls at midnight is not a matter of utmost importance — let me add that midnight here means 12.00 o'clock official time, during the period of summer time but not later.... People are asked to make a sacrifice that will bring some sinner back to penance or give strength to a young man in Poland or Czechoslavakia to stand firm and shed his blood for the faith.

This pastoral was penned by a bishop considered mild by comparison with some of his way-out contemporaries: Dr Joseph Walsh, Archbishop of Tuam. Some made dancing after midnight in Lent a mortal sin. The hilarious Bishop O Callaghan of Clogher threw in selling the *United Irishman* and collecting for An Cumann Cabhrach (Prisoners' Dependants Fund) to keep company with membership of the IRA, poitín-making, perjury, attendance at non-Catholic services and dancing after midnight in Lent. The only growth-industry — the only industry — seemed to be the creation of new areas of sinfulness.

The Archbishop of Tuam was also concerned about company keeping of a different kind:

> In recent years the occasions of sin have been multiplied. The old Irish dances have been discarded for foreign

importations which, according to all accounts, lend themselves not so much to rhythm as to low sensuality. Company keeping under the stars at night has succeeded in too many places the good old Irish custom of visiting, chatting and storytelling from one house to another, with the rosary to bring all home in due time.

And as to obedience, the irrepressible Dr O'Doherty of Galway had this pithy advice for fathers: "If your girls don't obey you, if they are not in at the hours appointed, lay the lash upon their backs."

When the first attempt to liberalise the Sunday drinking hours failed, the hierarchy, in 1950, drew attention to ecclesiastical law on Sunday opening and said: "So long as this ecclesiastical law remains it would be sinful to agitate for their opening. . . . " Yet another sin for the seemingly endless list.

Does hindsight make the 50s bleaker than the period actually was? Let the following extracts from a local paper in Mayo answer that question simply:

> 1957 is gone and may all our bad luck go with it. It was a gloomy and depressing year. . . . Roughly an average of 60,000 were unemployed every week, while emigration took as big a toll as ever of the cream of the youth. . . . Typical of the unchristian treatment of those employed in Mayo is the road worker whose weekly income is a little over £5.0.0 . . . .

On the Commemoration of St Patrick's Day the same paper, in its editorial, summed up the state of the country:

> Instead of being a day of rejoicing, of pride and of intense patriotism; instead of becoming an Irish-Ireland day in the true sense of the phrase, St Patrick's Day has been a dull, listless, uninspiring day for the youth and one of sad, nostalgic yearning for the aged and all those remembering the stirring events, the celebrations at the

turn of the century and later, when an alien government ruled the roost and it was not popular to be Irish.

Just now when there is so much pessimism, cynicism, defeatism and despair in Ireland there was never more need of a resurgence or an awakening to the fact that it is we as a people who are slipping or have slipped — not the nation.

These were the years when writers came from abroad to record the last will and testament of what became known as "The Vanishing Irish". Even the bishops got in on that particular act, particularly Dr Lucey of Cork — the man who gave the confirmation sermon a new lease of life to the intense annoyance of the politicians. Lucey declared: "Rural Ireland is stricken and dying and the will to marry and live off the land is gone." The miracle was that anyone who was free to go anywhere abroad stayed to attend what was surely going to be a badly-attended wake.

The tale of decline can be summed up in a minimum of statistics. The census of 1951 showed the first increase in population since 1841, despite the fact that an average of 25,000 emigrated every year between 1946 and 1951. But by 1956 the population had declined to the lowest level ever recorded and the rate of emigration had risen to 40,000 a year. By 1957 the rate of emigration and the birth-rate were running neck and neck.

It was against this background that Noel Browne launched his campaign to rid the country of the killer disease tuberculosis, and then do battle with the Bishops, the Irish Medical Association, the politicians who were supposed to assist him, those who chose to be mute and enjoy the political scrummage and, eventually — the Old Sow having peculiar ways with the more wayward of her farrow — with his own vision of what he came to regard as his own martyrdom.

"Hit me now with my Mother and Child in my arms!"

10

"Hit me now with my Mother and Child in my arms!"

While Fianna Fáil retired to its winter quarters to re-organise and plan strategy the Coalition Government showed every sign of being, in the immortal words of Patrick Kavanagh about the Iniskeen football team, "ball-hungry". In the war he had declared on tuberculosis Dr Browne was giving an impression of perpetual motion. With the aid of the new drugs which were just coming into use, and by pushing rapidly ahead with the building of sanatoria (assisted by money diverted from the Irish Hospitals Sweepstakes), as well as a highly-professional publicity campaign, he did more than anyone else in government to convince a battered population that pressing problems could be solved.

As most of his education was received in England he had almost no knowledge of Irish. Despite his lack of ministerial experience and the formidable tasks facing him, he managed to master the language in a matter of months. Soon he was broadcasting in Irish as part of the health publicity campaign. For the first and only time in the history of the state a minister was actually giving the language the importance in reality that the Constitution gave it in theory.

His decision to live up to what he considered to be his constitutional obligation brought its own reward. The Connemara Gaeltacht, which he began to visit regularly at this time, was to become a constant in a turbulent career crammed with contradictions.

The Fianna Fáil Government had brought in the Health Act of 1947 as the basis of a badly-needed health service. Being particularly concerned by the high rate of infant mortality in Ireland at this time, Dr Browne decided to introduce maternity treatment and medical attention for children up to the age of sixteen, free of charge and without any means test. This was essentially what the Mother and Child Scheme was about.

For anyone who wishes to understand fully the various complications, inconsistencies and misunderstandings surrounding this first public confrontation between Church and State (not forgetting, as is frequently the case, the vested medical interest), Professor J. G. Whyte's book, *Church and State in Modern Ireland: 1923-1979*, traces its background and development with scholarly detachment but in the manner of a well-constructed political thriller.

He has also brought to light an interesting point about the initial public health legislation in 1945. This was handled by Dr Con Ward for the Fianna Fáil Government and was attacked in the Dáil on the grounds that it contravened Christian principles and that it would not meet with the approval of the Catholic hierarchy. The main attack came from Deputies Costello, McGilligan and Mulcahy of Fine Gael and seemed to be part of a growing tendency in Dáil Eireann to put party political advantage ahead of every other consideration. Fine Gael were far from being the only offenders but in this instance the issues they raised came back to haunt them.

These attacks caused Dr Ward, who was a religious man, to approach the Archbishop of Dublin, Dr McQuaid, privately for advice. In the second of two letters to the Parliamentary Secretary the Archbishop described the proposed legislation as "substantially good'. However, this public health bill, which the Irish Medical Association found little fault with, never became law. Fate, in the shape of the Monaghan bacon factory, intervened and a justifiably disgruntled Dr Ward left public life.

Dr Jim Ryan, the Irish politician who brought the

practice of inarticulation to the level of an art form, took over the handling of a new health bill which was essentially the same as Dr Ward's, particularly in the provision for a mother and child scheme. Now, however, Fine Gael seemed happy with the proposals (Fianna Fáil folklore has it that it was an exceptionally busy time in the courts and the lawyers were otherwise occupied) but the doctors were unhappy and the Hierarchy registered an official protest against the proposals for a mother and and child scheme.

Although the 1947 proposals were essentially the same as those of 1945 the Church seemed to detect a move towards undue state intervention in family medical matters: one of the Church's main spheres of influence. The war was over and the world was returning to normal and Ireland would again be susceptible to disturbing trends from abroad.

It is the considered opinion of two generations of begrudgers that the medical profession alerted the Church to dangers, moral in both instances, but in one instance the morality had distinct financial attributes. One was spoken, the other unspoken. It was another example of the organised lay Catholics getting out there and putting pressure on the Church to put pressure on the politicians, on the doctors and on the laity, who would in turn ... it would take a clever and exceedingly alert person to tell his arse from his elbow in that kind of scrimmage. Poor Noel Browne!

James Dillon challenged certain proposals in the legislation, concerning compulsory medical examination, in the courts on the grounds of their unconstitutionality; and there are neither gold watches nor free holidays in Butlins for those who guess who got places on his legal team. James Dillon, to his credit, was against compulsion in all matters; although older begrudgers recall that the live-in apprentices in Monica Duff's were expected to say the Rosary aloud each night. And good enough for them too, if they were!

His intervention enabled de Valera to reply to the Bishops' complaint by saying that the constitutionality of the legislation was now in question. At this stage the February 1948 election was over and the ball was heading for the Coalition's court. But the obvious point is that it was exceedingly strange that the confrontation with the bishops and the doctors, when it came, seems to have taken so many people who ought to have been fully aware of the pitfalls so badly on the wrong foot. It is, perhaps, as well to note that the Coalition was not brought down by the Dr Browne resignation, although that romantic gloss has crept into history. The government fell when some rural Independents turned their backs on it for failing to increase the price of milk.

Before he knew what really hit him, Dr Browne was in conflict with the Irish Medical Association (always regarded as a posse of not so silent and not holy Knights), the Bishops, all his fellow-ministers and his Taoiseach; not forgetting his party leader who was eventually asked by the Taoiseach to request his Minister for Health' resignation: a trick which obviously slipped Garret FitzGerald's mind when he tried to shift his Minister for Health in 1986.

Any one of these opponents was heavyweight eliminator material; not even Cassius Clay in his hey-day could have hoped to handle two out of four and win. But in defeat Noel Browne had one glorious round which won him his permanent place in the record books. For the first time in the history of the state, anyone who could read and who had the price of a newspaper got the inside story of what happened when the Church set out to bend politicians to its will. It was all there because Browne had made the necessary arrangements with the editor of the *Irish Times* and that ensured that all the other papers carried the correspondence also.

It has been said frequently about that episode that Dr Browne was raw and inexperienced in negotiations, that he was vain, that he fought on too many different fronts, that he was incapable of responding to party or cabinet discipline except by displays of petulance and that only by agreeing that he was always right, even when he was contradicting something he had earlier asserted, could anyone get on with him.

It is just because he lacked the so-called virtues these deficiencies seem to indicate that he succeeded in doing what he did: break the rules of the Lodge and emerge screaming that the Emperor had not a stitch between him and his maker.

This has nothing got to do with the rights and wrongs of the case; it has everything to do with the manner in which the business of the state was conducted. He provided the evidence to support what every thinking citizen in the country suspected: that we had a Catholic Constitution for a people who could either like it or lump it. All pressure groups have equal rights when it comes to exercising what political muscle they possess; the problem was that in this respect the Catholic Church was much more equal than others. Those readers who may equate recent happenings in our native land with the events of 1951 should ask themselves one serious question: is it the elected representatives, who constantly laud our brand of parliamentary democracy, or the non-elected pressure groups who are bringing politics into disrepute and causing so many people to abstain from voting on important issues?

Time has shown many things clearly, among them that Noel Browne is incapable of remaining for long inside any party structure, even one created by himself. Yet only inside the parliamentary system did he seem to find an outlet for his charismatic talents. Like many another, hindsight makes his heart grow harder.

He joined Fianna Fáil, after Labour had rejected him as too hot a political potato; just like the Annuities in the 30s. He supported Fianna Fáil legislation which resembled his own beloved Act as near as made little difference and spent years as a member of the party (being at one time joint National Treasurer), leaving only when Seán MacEntee refused to have him as a running-mate for the good reason that Browne would have taken his seat.

Years later, in an interview with a far from demanding

journalist, he denounced Fianna Fáil for having emasculated the mother and child legislation at the behest of the bishops. In fact it was Paddy McGilligan, knowing that the Catholic hierarchy had written a letter of protest concerning the Fianna Fáil Government (which was later withdrawn from the newspapers after negotiations but copies were available around Dublin) who complained in the Dáil that the Bishops were letting Fianna Fáil get away with things they had hammered Fine Gael for.

Being right at all times about all things is an obsession with Noel Browne, but he is not material for any begrudger to spread himself on. More than any contemporary politician Noel Browne's heart is very close to the heart of Ireland. The ordinary voting public always sensed that instinctively.

There now followed an arid and dreary period in Irish politics. As other countries showed signs of recovering from the ravages of war, this island sank deeper into despondency. Fianna Fáil got back into power but the party began to resemble an old-folks outing to the big smoke with the younger backbenchers pushing the elderly ministers in wheelchairs.

One government's innovations were thrown out by the next one in the manner of unruly boys kicking over one another's sandcastles at the seaside. The Irish News Agency was killed before it was really established. The aircraft purchased by one government for the trans-Atlantic service were sold by another as an exercise in economic propaganda. One government bought a short-wave transmitter to give — wait for it — "Ireland's message to the world". The next government sold it to Pakistan; which was really like applying for relegation to the non-professional league.

James Dillon, who had reverted to his earlier role as a begrudger, suggested that the shortwave transmitter be converted into knitting-needles to be distributed to the women of the Shannon area of Clare. He maintained that the rabbits who would eventually take over the runways to play leap-frog could be shorn and their hair knitted into jerseys.

So low had the national morale fallen that when two emissaries from the Pakistan Government came into Radio Eireann requesting permission to inspect the transmitter the receptionist rang a senior executive in horror shouting, "Hurry on down here, will you? There are men here with turbines on their heads and they say they want to buy the station".

Even the idea of a Coalition fell into disrepute as a lone Fine Gael TD in a three-seat constituency found out in the election of 1957. With the assistance of his Clann na Talún partner he had taken a seat from Fianna Fáil in the "Keep Them Out" election. Now he stuck manfully to the instruction, "Vote 1 and 2 for your Coalition candidates in order of your choice", and assumed that his partner was doing likewise.

On polling day his Clann na Talún partner called to his house and invited him to come on a tour of polling stations. There was a market on in the first town and being slightly dehydrated they slipped into the back of a pub for a discreet and illegal drink. A man joined them out of the dim recesses of the pub and addressed the Clann na Talún TD by his christian name.

"Yerra, good morning, Martin," said the TD, "Pull him a pint, Mick. Did you vote yet?"

"Indeed I did. Mary and myself must have been dam near the first two to vote here above."

To the embarrassment of the Fine Gael TD, who had been educated by the Holy Ghost Fathers some distance from home, his partner pursued the matter further.

"And how did you vote?"

"Well, it's like this," said Martin, "Every turn until this second last time out you got the two strokes in our house. But then there was this business of a Coalition, so Mary gave you the stroke and I gave it to your friend here."

"Well, fuck you for a contrary bollix! Cancel that pint, Mick!"

When he told the story later the Fine Gael TD said that the sinking feeling he got was exceeded only by the feeling he experienced the following evening when he lost both his seat and his deposit. The matter had little to do with political philosophy, or even personalities, but a lot with constituency geography. There was one big town in the constituency and that was where he lived and that was why he was chosen as part of the "Put Them Out" campaign. Up to then the town votes were regarded as "loose fish", in the words of Herman Melville, and it was a tradition that there never was a town candidate. Now that the interesting experiment in political development was over it was time to dump him in case he got ideas above the station in life others had ordained for him. Only himself and poor Martin, who was clearly a gom, were unaware of the conspiracy.

The incident, in which only the names have been concealed, illustrates a certain gentlemanly innocence in the practice of politics which was the hallmark of Fine Gael for many years after 1932. For instance, the deposed "townie" did not find out for years after his departure from politics that his fellow-TDs had almost all the postmen in the constituency on what was known locally as a "porter-levy".

The postmen held back all letters informing people that they were going to get the old-age pension or other state benefit to which age and circumstances entitled them. They then rang their chosen patron and informed him that a call to certain houses was in order, to inform people that "the job is oxo and the letter should be here tomorrow".

Lenin said that one of his missions in life was to abolish the village idiot. It is just as well, for the sake of many of our pillars of rural democracy, that Comrade Lenin's writ never ran in Ireland. But, as the old saying has it, "If you can't bate 'em join 'em", and there arose in the County of Galway — or thereabouts — a retired salesperson of soured and flavoured milk who said, "I shall arise and make Fine Gael so professional in the practice of chicanery that

Fianna Fáil will be reduced to tapping one another's telephones to find out where the ill wind is blowing and who it is who is blowing it, saving your presence." But that is another day's work. . . .

In 1959, at the age of 77, de Valera ran for the Presidency and won. Even in what was to be his second last electoral hurrah, he tried to deal the people one off the bottom of the pack. He staged a referendum to abolish PR to coincide with the presidential election: "Vote Dev and Yes" was the slogan. But as a wag said at the time, the people stuck with the devil they knew in both contests. Fianna Fáil tried one more time to dump PR but with the assistance of some imaginative speculation on television the straight vote got clobbered again.

If Seán Lemass behaved like a man in a hurry once he got his hands on the tiller it was because he seemed to know that his time would be limited. It has been truly said of him that he came to power too late and left it too soon; although his abrupt departure, leading to an unsatisfactory succession which has cast its shadow over the party ever since, has never been satisfactorily explained.

But he was a lucky Taoiseach. He was the obvious successor to de Valera, who held on to power far too long because he hated to give it up and even refused to resign as Taoiseach until the votes in the presidential election were counted. It reminds one of Christy Ring's famous advice to young hurlers: "Never take your eye off the ball, even if the referee has it. Play the game for the game's sake and if your opponent should receive an injury let it be accidental." One feels that had de Valera taken up hurling instead of rugby his advice would not have been much different.

Lemass was also lucky that his coming to power coincided with a period of world growth and economic recovery. For this he could not and did not claim any credit. But he had prepared the plan, with the assistance of T. K. Whitaker, and the blessing of de Valera who was still Taoiseach. Lemass was not afraid to reverse policies he had previously preached and implemented, particularly as they had failed spectacularly to create employment, develop our natural resources, stem emigration and give people hope.

It must be said that in the particular kingdom of darkness that was Ireland in the late 50s the man who produced a white stick would be acclaimed as a wonder-worker. Lemass produced a stick and a seeing-eye dog and the rising tide that floats all ships can be thanked for the rest of a recovery which was only temporary and fraught with fatal flaws. But at least the ship had been refurbished, refitted and caulked and it did float free of the dismal mud-flats.

Lemass was a particular kind of patriot, and it is a pity, in view of the present petrified state of the country, that he is popularly portrayed as a kind of Chairman of Ireland (Inc.). That he also was, to an extent, but he did under-stand that which — for want of better words — can be called motivating factors. He came as close as he ever did to articulating his basic philosophy in a Dáil speech shortly after becoming Taoiseach:

> Personally, I believe that national progress of any kind depends largely upon an upsurge of patriotism — a re-vival of patriotism, if you will — directed towards constructive purposes. Patriotism, as I understand it, is a combination of love of country, pride in its history, traditions and culture, and a determination to add to its prestige and achievements.

This was what people had been waiting to hear for a long time: the country does have a future, material prosperity can be achieved west of Dún Laoire Pier and Dublin Airport.

As the country changed so too did Fianna Fáil. All of a sudden the wheelchair brigade were in the county home (not Seanad Eireann, in case of confusion and offence), some protesting more loudly than others that they could feel young hands measuring them in the night for habits and coffins, for some of them still retained their Dáil seats.

The mighty party machine was taken over by Blaney, Boland, Haughey, O'Malley (the uncle) and Lenihan. Frank Aiken was the last to go, his semblance of an even-handed foreign policy shattered by Lemass's pragmatic praise for the USA as the guardian of all we stood for against the Eastern hordes who were all up for the other thing.

It was all pragmatism now, all right. It was always either one thing or another. Like poor ex-President Ford who, according to Lyndon B. Johnson, was so retarded mentally that he could not chew gum and fart at the same time, Ireland had tacked away from the land where her old heroes slept and was heading somewhere on automatic pilot: up a fjord as we were to discover later.

But they were exciting times. To see the Donegal Mafia organising a bye-election campaign in a place like Kerry was to experience a real-life liberation of Guam by John Wayne and the usual extras. It was all dark glasses, chewing-gum, screeching tyres and staccato commands in a language, as Queen Elizabeth 1 said of Shane O'Neill, "like the howling of a dog". Not everyone in Fianna Fáil was overjoyed. Soft-voiced Dr Hillery was known to refer to them as the "Black and Decker Brigade", and Jack Lynch believed that the discreet distribution of rubber boots to farmers, courtesy of the Real O'Brien who shifts things, would have a greater bearing on results than the histrionics of the Swilly Shock Troops.

To ensure that the new-found prosperity (which was going to last forever) was going to nail Fianna Fáil firmly in power a kind of charitable institution called Taca Fáil was founded — quickly abbreviated to Taca. It was a form of planned giving which guaranteed Fianna Fáil protection for those who paid hundreds of pounds to eat tired chicken and ham in the right company.

As was his wont, O'Malley (the uncle with the charisma) did not beat about the bush about the real purpose of Taca: "I have no hesitation, all things being equal, in supporting people who support me and us."

Taca eventually became an embarrassment, even to the hardest necks in Fianna Fáil, and more discreet ways of extracting money from those who believed in charity beginning and staying at home were found. The country became aware of this when Charlie Haughey took over the party and had a bit of bother getting the key of the money-box from some pro-Lynch (that should really read "O'Malley, the nephew") begrudgers in Burlington Road.

Because Irish is the first language of the state nobody, not even those who were paying dearly for the bad food, understood what Taca meant. In the Dáil one day, Seán Dunne of Labour and Michael Carty of Fianna Fáil did a two-hander on it with the assistance of Dr Dinneen's Dictionary:

> *Mr Dunne: Taca* is defined as follows: a peg, pin or nail; an item of rigging, a fastening, a foothold, security, one who can be relied on to do a thing.
> *Mr Carty:* Is mór an taca dúinn tú.
> *Mr Dunne:* An impediment to speech.
> *Mr Carty:* Níl an rud sin ortsa, bail ó Dhia ort.
> *Mr Dunne:* If you use the aspirate it also means a want, defect, isolation. That is Taca. What does the other half of the title mean, according to Dr Dinneen?
> *Mr Carty:* Destiny.
> *Mr Dunne: Fáil:* a hedge, a dead hedge, a protection, a paling or wall, bedclothes, a covering, a circle, a fold, a pound, a barrier, a legal bar, an obstacle.

While most commentators agree that Lemass favoured short Cabinet and Fianna Fáil party meetings, not everyone agrees that this resulted in greater efficiency. Dr Tod Andrews, for instance, was of the opinion that Lemass was not able to control his young ministers and allowed them to run their ministries as if they were their private fiefs.

He may have had his own devious reasons for allowing Donogh O'Malley — if indeed he did allow him — to announce the introduction of free second-level education without first informing the Minister for Finance. If he had, Jack Lynch certainly did not seem to appreciate them.

One could go on, for politics, even in Mary Horan's country, is a hard old station. Despite the exertions of handlers, public relations executives, commentators with hidden axes to grind, teachers of false television sincerity and all others who seek to give the public a bum steer, the whole person appears in the fullness of time. Time does tell and murder will out.

Try as one may, one cannot have Lemass the convert to free enterprise, the man who reversed the flow of emigration, architect of the New Ireland, welcome antidote to the embroidered Fáinne on Dev's cloak — all that and more you cannot have without accepting Taca, the vulgarisation of Ireland, the destruction of Dublin and the failure to develop the country's real resources; apart, perhaps, from tourism which is always a mixed blessing in any civilised country.

Even the most regurgitated cup of tea in Irish history, unless its purpose was to blow Terence O'Neill away with Orange bombs, served no other purpose in the long run. It was a nice gesture, most appreciated by those who believe that wisdom resides in newspaper headlines, of faith without good works. Politically, or even physically, Lemass was taking far less of a risk than Dan Breen took when he entered the Dáil ahead of Fianna Fáil.

Still, when the 50th anniversary of the Rising of 1916 was commemorated both President de Valera and Taoiseach Lemass, who had taken their chances then and lived to tell the tale, could at least take some pleasure in the fact that the state had survived and seemed to show signs of thriving. Its true potential was still unrealised, the Proclamation of 1916 still remained "a fine piece of writing", but the freedom to achieve real freedom was a lot stronger than it was when Seán Lemass, not yet sixteen, had joined the Volunteers.

The Commemoration of 1916 was as fulsome as all subsequent remembrances have been almost non-existent.

The newly-arrived television service played its part but fears that the commemorations would lead to yet another assault on the fourth green field proved groundless. People were too busy having a good time, and apart from a baton-charge in O'Connell Street when the gardaí attacked a Sinn Féin march returning from Glasnevin Cemetery, there was no blood spilt. Copies of the Proclamation were distributed to every school in Ireland where they still hang, unread and irrelevant.

Neither Lemass, nor the man who was to succeed him, could have foreseen that within a decade some Irish politicians, with the assistance of some historians of amazing flexibility, would launch an attack on the Rising and those who organised it, and offer what amounted to certificates of illegitimacy to the State and its citizens. Contemporary history had to be adjusted in the interests of something which has become unclear. It could have been something as simple as "Vingince, be Jasus", but it matters little now. It was only another manifestation of that most useless of Irish institutions, 'The Great National Debate": the original lighthouse in a bog, diverting when it shines but serving no practical purpose.

Lemass has been credited with originating the "Let's Face It" phase of political development, which is unfair to Jack Lynch, the first reluctant Taoiseach. "Let's Face It" means that there is no solution to any problem apart from that offered by striking the best temporary bargain with the nearest available devil. In other words, "Let's Face It" is the accepted preface to a cop-out.

First there was the succession race which was not a succession race at all, for we are now asked to believe that Lynch was Lemass' chosen successor: it was just that his signals were not understood for a number of years. If this is truly the case, Lemass thought a lot more of de Valera than some would have us now believe. For Jack Lynch was straight out of the "laughter of comely maidens" scenario rewritten by any sentimental male-orientated Munster writer you can recall: Con Houlihan will do nicely.

Seán O Ríordáin, who was at school with Lynch in the North Mon (and was a cute Cork hoor in his own right, albeit of the non-practising variety) explained what power meant to Lynch in a brilliant essay in the *Irish Times* entitled "Narcissus".

Its theme was simple: Narcissus was in love with the idea of having power, not to do anything on God's earth with it if he could help it, but to make sure it was not snatched by the wrong hands. Years after O Ríordáin wrote, as power began to ebb away from Narcissus, he behaved as the astute poet had foreseen. Even as these words are being written ... but that is an unworthy thought which will be banished this instant.

However, it is simply not true that Jack Lynch did not have a vision of Ireland, just as de Valera and Seán Lemass did. Lynch's Ireland revolved around the Munster Final. The week would pass in honest but not too exhausting work and much speculation about the outcome. The weekend would be devoted to the Great Hosting. Drink would be consumed in manly moderation, before and after the Great Event, and songs would be sung in orderly but forthright fashion. "The Banks", "The Bould Thady Quill" and "An Poc ar Buile" would make the rafters ring but any troublemaker who struck up "We Shot 'em in Pairs comin' down the Stairs' would be immediately handed over to an understanding constabulary. ("Just a few thumps, Sergeant, he just can't hold it."). On Monday morning honest work and reasonable discussion on what had passed and what was still there to play for would be resumed.

For there would be a Munster Final every week in Jack Lynch's Ireland — two or three at Christmas and Easter if things were going well: if there were no unseemly strikes, if all injuries had been inflicted accidentally and all disagreements settled on the field out of the referee's sight. ...

Alas, poor Lynch! The weather and the times should really have kept in tune with his rosy, sweetly-scented vision of the Ireland of crushed grass, mature Paddy and "the wicked chuckle of hurleys" in the Tipperary square:

the Ireland where the safe period meant the teams and the crowd standing to attention and facing the flag for the National Anthem.

Just when everyone thought that the fourth green field and its inhabitants had settled down to enjoy prosperity like everyone else the most shocking row broke out and before you could say "Paisley" there were guns, or rumours of guns, and hurleys were being used by punishment squads to break legs and Jack Lynch's Fianna Fáil would never be the same again. And Jack Lynch's Ireland, which existed in a state of peaceful neutrality — somewhere south of a line from Dublin to Clifden — began to fall apart.

11

Why does nobody like the Northern Loyalists?

Now that we have at last got around to the Northern Unionists something very sad must be said right away: they are not loved by very many people. In fact, one gets the impression that many of the more prominent members of the tribe do not get on that well among themselves.

Let's face it, does James Molyneaux really like Ian Paisley? Is Ian Paisley constantly in fear of finding Peter Robinson thinking behind his back? Can Robinson bear Harold McCusker? Can anyone on earth, even Conor Cruise O'Brien before his fateful meeting with the synagogue cat, put up with John Taylor?

Even in the country that gave them the big boot and the loan of the big foot to go with it, they have very few friends, as the recent Westminster debate on the Hillsborough Agreement showed; and some of the friends they have they would be far better off without. Apart from the Afrikaners, whom they superficially resemble to a frightening degree, the Unionists must be the most unsympathetic white national minority on the face of the earth. A large part of their problem is that they are neither British nor Irish, in their own eyes, and despite being given a little sectarian state where they were going to form a perpetual majority they continued to behave like a national minority. Those who could help them to overcome this basic problem they refused to talk to except when issuing curt instructions about how their lives were going to be run.

It must be said that this lack of sympathy and understanding goes back a long time, as far as the non-Unionist part of the island is concerned. A writer from the province of Connacht, writing shortly after the State of Northern Ireland was established, had this to say of them:

They have remained so illiterate and barbarous, that whenever one of them becomes civilized, or even partly civilized, he is forced to flee from his environment, lest he may be devoured by his neighbours. Even as far back in our history as two or three thousand years, when there was a Pictish aristocracy ruling Ulster, an Ulsterman was refused his spurs as a knight until he had murdered (and very possibly devoured) a Connachtman. Those Picts, however, produced a literature which we honour. The present caste, during their period of rule in Ulster, have produced nothing in a cultural sense other than a barbarous rite, which consists of beating a drum savagely with bare fists until the blood spurts from the wrist veins. The Picts produced the Ulidian Sagas, Cuchulainn, the Red Branch Knights. They imposed their culture on the rude Gaelic savages that invaded Ireland, presumably from the country that is now called England. The Gaels in turn became highly cultured, and when they were defeated by the Normans, they imposed their high culture on the rude Norman savages. The Normans in their turn became cultured, but alas, when they were overthrown by the succeeding invasions of Anglo-Saxons, Hessians and Lowland Scots, they did not impose their assimilated Gaelic culture. Instead of the Red Branch Knights, the Anglo-Saxon and Lowland Scottish ruling caste in Ulster have merely produced the Orange Order. The only poetry of this knighthood consists of a few scurrilous illiterate poems. Their drama consists of an annual mock battle in which nobody is killed, but in which everybody gets drunk. Now, however, that the working class of Ulster is beginning to revolt against the barbarous tyranny of its illiterate rulers, we hope that the province may become once more an honour to our community.

That last fond hope, expressed so optimistically there by Liam O'Flaherty, was one that sustained many republican socialists, up to and including the present day. The trouble was, and still remains, that the vast majority of working class Unionists see themselves as being a cut above their Catholic counterparts because they are part of the ruling caste. Cannonfodder for ambitious politicians they may be but that is not their own perception of themselves. Apart from that, class solutions to a problem that is sectarian and tribal in essence are unreal as well as being many decades out of date. Divisions in Northern Ireland stem from many sources but power, and the tradition of having almost unlimited power, is the principal one.

It is not our intention to weary you with a recital of recent events with which you are already familiar from the acres of press reports and articles, television films and discussions, radio documentaries and even works of fiction. But a few loose ends need to be tidied up. Much earlier we mentioned the Boundary Commission which was established under the Treaty of 1922. Its purpose was to examine the border between the two states for the purpose of re-drawing it in certain places. Lloyd George assured the Irish signatories, privately, that such large tracts would be returned to the Free State — areas where Catholics were in a clear majority — that economic reality would ensure that the Northern State could not endure.

The Unionists knew how to deal with that threat which was not a real threat at all. They ignored the Commission and a South African judge was sent in as their substitute. An inspired leak to a newspaper indicated that the Commission was not going to change anything worth speaking of and the Free State Government was forced to withdraw in disarray. The Unionists now had everything they wanted, more or less, and proceeded to run the place as they wished. Britain did not want to know and as there was a parliament in Stormont awkward questions could not be raised in Westminster.

Using the excuse that they were in constant danger of invasion from the south and that the Catholic population were not to be trusted, the Unionists armed themselves with guns, a three-tier armed police force and a variety of Special Powers. The majority of Catholics, their expectations dashed by the Civil War in the south and the collapse of the Boundary Commission in 1924, terrified by the assassination squads which were never apprehended (for the very good reason that they operated with the aid of the so-called security forces), found themselves isolated and abandoned. At best they gave but a sullen recognition to the institutions of the state which they found impossible to ignore. A small percentage of them supported the IRA which had very little water in which to swim outside of Derry and Belfast.

But the IRA was not a great source of worry to the Stormont Government, although it was a very useful bogeyman when a bogeyman was required. The Government had many other things on its mind, chief among them in the beginning being how to increase even further its grip on a state in which it had a carefully-created majority calculated to last for generations — which was why the missing three counties of Ulster were allowed to go missing. But being of a nervous disposition the Unionists decided to reduce the little power the Catholic minority had still further.

Gerrymandering gets its name from Elbridge Gerry who, as Governor of Massachusetts in 1812, carved up Essex County so as to give maximum advantage to the Republican party. Someone said the map looked like a salamander and the obvious change was made. The new word came into its own in Northern Ireland. Derry City was the example most quoted. Here, an electorate two-thirds Catholic (and Nationalist) and one-third Protestant (and Unionist) elected a Corporation two-thirds Unionist and one-third Catholic. This miracle was achieved by placing 87% of the Catholics in one ward which returned eight seats, while 87% of the Protestants were placed in two wards and returned twelve seats.

When this particular chicken came home to roost in 1968 many people in the Republic were puzzled by the slogan "One man, one vote", which goes to show that the Anti-Partition campaign was not even working well at home. Not only was gerrymandering practised but voting in local elections was confined to house-owners and tenants. However, property owners could have as many as six votes, depending on valuation of property. No marks are awarded for guessing who the main property-owners in Derry were.

In 1971 Lord Brookeborough was interviewed by the *Guardian* about discrimination against Catholics in Derry. "That well might be," he said, "I don't know about that one. I don't know the answer to that. I believe it came somewhere near the truth, but I never came up against it."

But surely, a man who was Prime Minister of Northern Ireland from 1943 until 1963 would have to know what was going on in Derry, the second largest city in the state?

"No. I say, I never came up against it. I was told this was so, but I never came up against it."

The previous year, when speaking to a reporter from Dublin about the future of the state, Lord Brookeborough said: "Everything will be back to normal very soon. We have got rid of the traitor." It was as simple as that: throw out Captain O'Neill, who only tried to buy a little time by granting too little far too late, and everything would automatically calm down again.

One has learned to accept prevarication, and even downright lies, from politicians and some semblance of balance from historians — even those who could be classified as "committed". Try this one for size: "Though they did not want home rule for Ulster *(sic)*, the Unionists made the best of the situation, and contrary to popular belief, they did genuinely try to create a non-sectarian state in which all citizens would enjoy equal rights."

Later in his book, *The Narrow Ground,* A.T.Q. Stewart, who practices his trade in Queens University, Belfast, is assailed by an attack of the Brookeboroughs: "Westminster guaranteed the rights of the minority, and if they were in any way infringed, then Westminster and not Stormont was culpable."

That seems to indicate that Britain did not blow the whistle when it saw the foul, but was a foul really committed?

The problem for historians of the future will be to discover why the civil rights demonstrations of 1968 unleashed a sectarian war of unparallelled dimensions, reopened the Irish question and led to a guerilla war between a vastly reinvigorated IRA and the British Army. They will hardly be satisfied that the answer is to be found in a cant phrase of the conflict 'Fifty years of Unionist misrule!'

When the British Government eventually blew the whistle, after several finger-waggings, and decided that arses were going to be kicked, so to speak, under joint supervision, how did Mr Stewart react? In the pages of the *Spectator* there was much squealing and gnashing of molars:

For Ulster Protestants, all was changed utterly on 15 November 1985. A terrible, unwished-for duty was born. Overnight the bickering between Unionists ceased. One no longer spoke of Unionists, but only of Protestants. Twenty years ago, they had a parliament, a government and a state (of sorts) within the United Kingdom. The Troubles (more accurately the English response to the Troubles, and basic misinterpretation of their real cause) deprived them of their government. Edward Heath deprived them of their parliament. And now Mrs Thatcher has in effect deprived them of their homeland, or at least the right to have any say in how it is to be governed. So engrained is the English habit of blaming all Ulster's troubles on the Protestants that it still continues, in spite of the fact that for nearly 20 years the English themselves have been in control. Make no mistake about it, the Protestants will be blamed yet again when the Treaty founders, as it must. This is scant consolation for people in Northern Ireland, whatever their allegiance. The Foreign Office, an organisation more sinister than the IRA, has created a device so ingenious that wherever the Protestants touch it, it will blow up in their faces.

You must agree, whatever your allegiance, that A.T.Q. Stewart is pure magic. With footwork like that displayed above, the selling of countless dummies and the side-step out of tight corners, he is a natural for the out-half berth on the Ulster Old Believers XV; the Pythagorean initials provide the touch of the "rale aul' decency".

There were some conforming Catholics in the public service and one of them has written a very good book about his life and times in the Stormont Civil Service. Patrick Shea, author of *Voices and the Sound of Drums,* was the son of an RIC-man (who later became Clerk of the Petty Sessions in Newry) from near Kenmare, Co. Kerry, who joined the police rather than emigrate to the USA as his brother and sister had done. Patrick Shea joined the civil service and rose through the ranks until he came to a standstill at a certain point in the Ministry of Education.

One day in 1958, the Permanent Secretary, R.S. Brownell, sent for him and after revealing details of promotion opportunities in which his name had figured (and which Shea, being an honourable man, does not reveal in his book), shook hands with him and said, "Because you are a Roman Catholic you may never get any further promotion. I'm sorry."

Ten years earlier Shea had seen Colonel Hall-Thompson resign as Minister of Education in strange circumstances. He had offended powerful influences in the Unionist Party and in the Orange Order (of which Hall-Thompson was a member) by introducing a bill which they thought was going to make life easier (in Shea's words) "for schools managed by people whose attitude to the Crown and the State of Northern Ireland was less than enthusiastic." Following discussions with representatives of the Orange Order the Minister resigned. Patrick Shea comments:

> For the rest of his life Hall-Thompson remained silent about the circumstances of his departure. I believe that if the inside story were known it would be seen to be no more creditable than the much-publicised account of the fall of Dr Noel Browne . . . . It could be that some of the Stormont people who cried "shame" at the goings-on in Dublin had themselves acquiesced in a not dissimilar exercise which led to the sacrifice of a decent man within their own ranks.

Patrick Shea got the promotion he had long deserved in 1969 when he was made Permanent Secretary of the Ministry of Education. He comments wryly: "When I moved to Education in December 1969 there seemed to be some hope (how ridiculous it all seems now) that the political unrest which had been disturbing our community might be coming to an end." He also makes another equally interesting comment concerning the attitude of the community which, at this stage, considered him an Uncle Tom: "Except for my good, kind friends the Dominican nuns, those in charge of the management of Catholic education in Belfast, whilst always correct and friendly on official occasions, showed almost no desire to have me in their company on their own ground. Perhaps I was being spoiled by the attention I was getting elsewhere, but I cannot remember being invited to visit a Catholic school in Belfast."

To get to the heart of the matter one question has to be answered: was the Northern State doomed from the start to burn out as "a failed entity"? At the risk of offending all practising Nationalists (as well as nationalists of a lighter hue) the answer is that it did not have to fail. There was a time in its history when what is now called an "internal solution" could — and probably would — have worked. To say that now is not to depend too much on hindsight: the signs were there at the time for anyone who cared to read them and the clearest sign was given by the IRA.

The 50s campaign was the IRA's last attempt to free the Six Counties and re-unite Ireland by attacking from the south. It was to be the last romantic fling. Some of the leaders actually contacted de Valera asking him to have official eyes closed to what was about to happen and getting the current version of the Anti-Partition speech as a reply. The campaign was marked by one of the largest funerals ever seen in what must be one of the most funeral-conscious countries in the world and by a ballad about the man who was being mourned, "Seán Sabhat of Garryowen", which cannot be played on RTE but which seems to have been adopted as a rallying song by the supporters of the Limerick soccer team. It could well prove to be the most enduring achievement of a campaign that achieved very little, militarily or politically.

Sinn Féin did emerge from political darkness in the 1957 general election, after Clann na Poblachta brought down the second Coalition with its dying kick for using the Offences Against the State Act against the IRA. They won four seats, all from Fianna Fáil and a Fianna Fáil-supporting Independent, but Fianna Fáil were still able to form a government. Sinn Féin, married to the absentionist policy from which they are still seeking a divorce, refused to take the seats and lost them again at the next election.

The military campaign failed because there was no support for it in the northern state. What little support there was fell to the imposition of internment, north and south, and the re-introduction of the Military Tribunals in the south in the early sixties when the campaign looked like coming to life again. The alacrity with which the bright young Minister for Justice moved was favourably commented on in Northern Ireland and in Britain. They had not yet learned of *his* Daddy's and Mammy's people, or of his subterranean Republican sympathies. Neither friend nor foe rushes to draw attention to that particular part of The Boss's National Record. "What a selective memory you have, Grandmother," as Little Red Riding Hood would say.

The success of internment in the mid-50s proved to be a disguised curse for Northern Ireland in the long run. When Brian Faulkner pleaded with the British Government for permission to use it in 1971, in a desperate gambler's throw to save Stormont, it exploded in his face and strengthened the IRA. It was ironic, in view of the voting tradition of the state, that the lists had not been revised for years and that men who were dead and buried were sought to be put out of harm's way "behind the wire".

Dessie O'Malley, shortly after his appointment as Minister for Justice, hinted that internment might be introduced in the Republic but according to the secretary of the Department of Justice, Peter Berry, this was merely a ploy to win Protestant votes in an election in Donegal. This is denied by O'Malley, but then he also asserted that Kevin Barry was shot, and unfortunately, Peter Berry is in heaven with Bishop Moriarty and the Fenians, including those he kept such a close eye on during his days at the department.

In February 1962 the IRA issued a statement admitting failure and clearly stating the central cause for its campaign's failure. It stated that the campaign was officially over and that arms were to be dumped.

"Foremost among the factors responsible for the ending of the campaign has been the attitude of the general public whose minds have been deliberately distracted from the supreme issue facing the Irish people — the unity and freedom of Ireland."

The statement reads like a death certificate, and it was said at the time that the IRA would never again be a force in the land, but as Professor David Harkness points out in his book, *Northern Ireland since 1920*, the central point of the IRA statement was not emphasised, or even noted, officially in the North. In the *Ulster Yearbook 1965* the failure of the campaign was referred to: "By contrast with the state of affairs in the 1920s, there was no civil strife and the IRA campaign evoked no reprisals. Attacks were largely limited to sporadic incursions by small isolated parties who crossed the border for a short distance and returned immediately to Irish Republic territory. Broadly speaking, the campaign had no important impact on the life of the community."

This was surely the time for the Unionists to look again at their "untrustworthy" minority and grant some of the civil rights which would have mattered a lot at the time but which were much too little, far too late, when they were eventually granted with bad grace and more or less at the point of a gun. This is where the state failed. Whatever the future holds for the Six Counties now there can be no return to the big boot, weighed down by the big British foot, on the necks of the Catholics of Northern Ireland. And at the risk of rubbing salt into the largely self-inflicted wounds of the Northern Loyalists, they certainly had it coming to them. Apart from anything else they produced the most witless bunch of so-called politicians outside of a comic opera. They actually succeeded in raising the IRA from the dead and turning it into a first-class instrument of terror.

There is no need to take any old begrudger's word for it. Professor Walter Laqueur teaches modern history in Tel Aviv University but apart from that, which one could only regard as a superb qualification, he is a recognised expert on guerrilla warfare and on terrorism from a distinctly British viewpoint. In a book written in the late 70s he has the following remarks about the IRA:

> What distinguishes the most recent phase of Irish terrorism from all previous outbreaks is on the one hand its greater efficiency and on the other, its even greater cruelty. Up to the days of Michael Collins, Irish terrorists almost always bungled their operations; there was

an appalling lack of secrecy, of discipline and of planning. Of late, Irish terrorists greatly improved in this respect, though it is, of course, also true that they have less reason to fear the British security forces, which could no longer respond as they had done in a less civilised age.

No! No! One at a time, please! Britain was not found guilty of using torture in Northern Ireland by the European Court of Human Rights, only of using brutal and degrading methods of trying to make prisoners talk. The line between "brutal and degrading" and "torture" may be fine enough to be invisible but the British have their verbal bogeymen too. Any Irish miscreant, who was sober enough to remember, knows that when "Kevin Barry" (sorry Mr O'Malley but we are trying to make a valid political point here) is sung in an English public house the row doesn't start until the words "English soldiers tortured Barry" ring out. Of course, the purpose of the exercise usually was to start the row which invariably followed.

Before returning to Northern Ireland's last chance of an agreed internal solution to its built-in internal problem, it may be as well to say that we abhor violence as we abhor sin but are greatly impressed by the theory that only violent means are capable of stamping it out. As we are still trying to puzzle that one out we shall return to that great white hope for reform and reconciliation, Captain O'Neill.

The events leading up to the foundation and siting of what was known as the New University of Ulster were not sufficiently dramatic to gain much attention even in the Republic. The committee on higher education was established in 1963, under the chairmanship of Sir John Lockwood. Two years later it announced that the new university was to be sited, not in Derry where Magee College was already established, but in Coleraine, a town with more obvious attractions for a state controlled by the Orange Order. There was not a single Catholic on the Lockwood Committee but it became known that that was as close to the west bank of the Bann as the real power allowed O'Neill to go.

A gigantic motorcade from Derry to Stormont, with the Protestant and Catholic Bishops travelling together, could not change that decision. There is no evidence that O'Neill considered the decision a matter of great principle. His problem was that for all the public relations he was as much a prisoner of the Orange Order as every Prime Minister before and after him, until Brian Faulkner saw a ray of light too late.

Strangely enough it was Faulkner who brought to the surface the well-concealed vein of viciousness which even suave O'Neills with stage-English accents possess.

As Faulkner arrived in London to plead unsuccessfully with Edward Heath for his failed parliament, a letter appeared in the *Times* which placed a sharp object between Faulkner's shoulder-blades. It was Captain O'Neill's contribution to the politics of "vingince, be Jasus". He should have produced his dagger earlier.

It is difficult now to imagine a time when the Civil Rights Movement was, in Eamonn McCann's words, "middle-class, middle-aged and middle-of-the-road". Difficult to realise that Gerry Fitt's head was opened by an RUC baton on the bridge in Derry in 1968. Difficult to resist the temptation to pick out the highlights, or what now seem to be highlights, and chart again what has been charted so frequently that repetition as well as the passage of time has tended to dull what seemed at the time too horrible even to contemplate.

To come to the point: the State of Northern Ireland is a failed entity and whatever the Hillsborough Agreement does not achieve it does signify that failure. In so far as a pattern can be discerned in British policy towards its wayward creation it is one of gradual erosion of Loyalist supremacy. It is taking the Loyalist politicians, whatever about the people, a long time to recognise this fact as a reality with which they will have to live. They may have to live with a lot worse. The British may well be moving ever so slowly towards disengagement. This may or may not lead to the civil war which Dr Conor Cruise O'Brien metronomically forecasts. That eventuality may be less of a consideration to the British than some Loyalist politicians imagine as they whistle their way past the cemetery gate. It has, after all, been a long and bloody road from the bridge at Derry to Hillsborough.

Far from being a central cause of the problem the IRA is very much a symptom and a creation and, as has been shown, very much at the mercy of its supply of swimming-water. Apart from anything else it is the SDLP's greatest ally, much as Mr Hume may try to act offended at the thought. It is to the SDLP what Captain Moonlight was to Parnell and the SDLP have not been slow to play that card to good effect.

The IRA is doing nothing now that the IRA in the past did not do, or attempt to do, with less efficiency. At the time of writing the airwaves are carrying condemnations of the latest manifestation of its campaign of violence: death-threats to those working for and servicing the security forces. The BBC carries interviews with the present Northern Secretary, Tom King, the present Minister for Justice, Alan Dukes, and the present President of Sinn Féin, Gerry Adams. They all say predictable things which are also broadcast on the BBC World Service in various languages. Mr Adams cannot broadcast on RTE because of Section 31 of the Broadcasting Act, but the people who possess radio sets can hear him on the other services mentioned.

Like the Anti-Partition campaign of yore, Section 31 of the Broadcasting Act is the Republic's substitute for a positive policy on the northern problem. As Lady Brett Ashley in *The Sun Also Rises* said about being a bitch, "It's what we kind of have instead of God".

Far from being a new departure, this IRA campaign is about as old as Captain Boycott, if not older. It is also as new as the War of Independence as Alan Dukes, who went to school to the Christian Brothers, should know. In 1920 in a small village in one of the most peaceful counties west of the Shannon, traders were instructed to stop dealing with the RIC barracks. One day, a woman who kept on delivering milk to the policemen was found by horrified neighbours with three pig-rings inserted in the most sensitive part of her body.

People who read the history of the War of Independence in this county are surprised to find that alleged spies seemed to request drowning as a method of execution; but not so surprised when they find that the IRA was suffering from a chronic shortage of ammunition. As has been said, all wars are filthy and vicious and the longer they go on the more vicious they become. It can be reasoned that the IRA campaign is not a lawful one, but it is no less real for that, and the thousands who are not shocked by the campaign to the extent that they vote for Sinn Féin, are not impressed by arguments about legality; certainly not in the State of Northern Ireland.

And what these thousands think is very important, for these people constitute the water in which the IRA swims and without which the IRA campaign could not survive today, as others failed to survive in the past. There is some evidence that the Hillsborough Agreement may be worrying the IRA more than they would ever admit: if it is seen by the Catholics to work, which it is certainly not at the moment. The Power Sharing Executive worried them for a time also, but it worried the Loyalists even more and with the aid of Harold Wilson they did for it.

Loyalists who fear a united Ireland, and who realise that they face disunity as well as friendlessness, would do well to observe the present Northern Secretary, Tom King. Anyone who uses the words "mindless violence" in connection with the IRA's campaign of terror is a fool and a fool Tom King certainly is. But he is worse than being just a common or garden fool. He is the kind of fool the British Government frequently send to a place out of which they intend to move and let the wogs fight it out between themselves in the higher branches of the trees.

What friends the Loyalists may have are on the island of Ireland. One hopes they find them before the tide once more ebbs from under their moored political keel.

They are truly their own worst enemies, which is one reason why those who are opposed to them find it so easy to laugh at their predicament. Political historian John Whyte, who was previously mentioned, summed up their situation in a sentence: "It is because Protestant distrusts Protestant, not just because Protestant distrusts Catholic that the Ulster conflict is so intense."

And what of the IRA capacity for survival? The American who has written the organisation's history, through good days and bad, sums up its present situation as follows:

> The day of the gun may, indeed, be gone as the cautious have insisted for years and with it the IRA: but the last fifty years have given ample evidence of the vitality of the Republican Movement, annually consigned to the boneyard of Irish history and annually appearing before Tone's grave to renew a dedication to an invisible Republic. There, even today, the small band of persistent men on the perimeter of Europe on the edge of events create for that one summer's day an atmosphere of hope, of possibility, of pure dedication. At least in these men's ears Ireland unfree shall never be at peace, nor shall they at least for this generation.

It seems a rather cautious forecast in an Ireland of crammed jails, empty of positive idealism and full of naked greed for material possessions: which brings us back to the part of Ireland that fears a British withdrawal as much as the Northern Loyalists fear it, and with even more reason.

12

How Jack Lynch tossed a coin and Fianna Fáil played with the wind

If the eruption in the North took Stormont and Westminster by surprise it shocked Dublin out of whatever its Anti-Partition policy was at the time: it seems to have been non-existent but that is still unclear. It was totally unprepared on all fronts. It did not even know what was going on inside the Civil Rights Movement in the North. The British Government had two excellent informers strategically placed inside the Irish Special Branch and the Special Branch had two informers on the IRA Army Council. After the split in the IRA, however, the two informers took the Official side and left the Branch (and the two British spies of course) at a disadvantage with the Provisionals.

When a well-intentioned Army Intelligence Officer, Captain James Kelly, took it upon himself to find out what the situation of the beleaguered Catholic communities in the North was, the Branch and the Department of Justice discovered a purpose in life and began to spy on him and on those with whom he associated.

Elected representatives of these communities came to Dublin and demanded arms to defend their streets. Some of them would not thank you one little bit today for reminding them of how they kicked doors and barged their way into radio and television studios and eventually forced a truly reluctant Jack Lynch into action. He set up a sub-committee — the matter involved was at best only junior hurling — told them to do the right thing and not to bother him too much as there was a lot of important senior stuff to be decided.

There were not a lot of options open to him. He could have told the emissaries from the North to go home to their communities and tell them to offer up their little bit of bother for the Holy Souls; he could have made it an international issue by sending in the Army and calling for United Nations intervention, as we have already outlined; or do what he did and offer up prayers to Michael Collins that everything would work out to the satisfaction of all involved. For, as far as Dublin was concerned, it was back to 1922 with a vengeance, although it took some years for that to dawn on most politicians; Britain did not reach that point until 1985.

The fact that the Arms Trial (as it is rather comically called for nobody ever found out who got "The Arms" in the end) is still considered to be of interest to anyone at all indicates how little real impact the Northern Ireland conflict had had in the Republic. It is of interest only because of its effect on Fianna Fáil. But, as Vincent Browne has argued in *Magill,* there should never have been a trial. It is significant that the jury acquitted those defendants who said they were involved in a matter they considered to be official Government policy, as well as those who said they were not involved at all. It seems very clear that anyone in the Cabinet who did not know what was going on, did not wish to know or was not concerned enough to find out.

The Taoiseach stood his ground first and assured the Cabinet that the fracas was over, no names had been taken and the players had more or less shaken hands. Then Liam Cosgrave arrived with an anonymous letter from the more senior of the two British spies in the Special Branch and said it was his patriotic duty to read it out in the Dáil. The beans were to be spilt, this was Central Council stuff, and Jack Lynch decided to strike. Among lots of other things he created Charlie Haughey's Republican image.

As for Liam Cosgrave's patriotic duty, it would be nice

to be able to take the story at its face value but the fact is that the poor man failed to leak the letter to no less than two newspapers and was running out of ideas. After that it was open season on muck-birds in Dáil Eireann; only the guns were missing. ...

Frank O'Connor described the Senate Debate on Censorship as a "long, slow swim through a sewage bed". The 1970 Dáil Debate on the alleged importation of arms was remarkable for the high level of personal insult, the exploitation of the affair for the lowest party political motives and the almost total absence of concern for the people who were in the eye of the problem: the Nationalist population of the Six Counties. It was probably Dáil Eireann's most disgusting display of ignorant buffoonery, much of it well-lubricated, and proof positive that bad and all as the country may be, it scarcely deserves most of its public representatives. Unfortunately, considerations of space limit us to some short extracts.

Mr Moore: The Taoiseach dealt with the whole matter in his speech. Fine Gael speakers said that he would not have acted if their leader had not got this anonymous letter.

Dr Byrne: We said he might not.

Mr Moore: I want to ask Deputy Cosgrave will he let me see the document from which he read the other night.

Dr Byrne: Why should he?

Mr Moore: Why should he not? He mentioned it in the House.

INTERRUPTIONS

Leas-Cheann Comhairle: Order.

Mr Moore: Deputy Cosgrave gave the impression that he was speaking from an official document sent to him by some anonymous scribe.

Mr Crinion: He knows who it came from.

Mr Moore: That is something else. Perhaps he would disclose to the House who sent it, if he knows.

Dr Byrne: Why should he?

Mr Moore: That is only fair. We want to honour this man. This man, acting in a public spirit, sent a letter to Deputy Cosgrave. I am sure he will get the plaudits of the country for his great act.

Mr M. O'Leary: We know the plaudits he would get from the Deputy's party.

Mr Moore: We cannot do this unless we know his name.

Mr Harte: Was Deputy Lenehan not a member of the Blueshirts when this happened?

Mr. J. Lenehan: I was not. You were not born, you low-down pig, at that time. You would not be taken into the Blueshirts as bad as they were.

Mr O'Higgins: You were.

Mr. J. Lenehan: I was not.

Mr O'Higgins: Yes you were.

Leas-Cheann Comhairle: Order.

Mr. J. Lenehan: I swear on my oath that I was not.

Mr O'Higgins: Yes you were.

Mr J. Lenehan: I was not. You were in the Four Courts and you were executing people.

Mr O'Higgins: I am recognising another Blueshirt.

Mr J. Lenehan: I was never a Blueshirt.

Occasionally the problem of partition crept into the debate but even when it did more pressing matters again took over, as in this extract.

An Taoiseach: I think the time has come again for me — although I should have thought it would be unnecessary — to state again Fianna Fáil's policy for the reunification of our country by peaceful means. That has been Fianna Fail policy since the foundation of our party and Fine Gael can claim no credit, as they seem to be doing of late, that it was they who suggested that this was the best means of securing reunification. I want to say too, Sir, that I have never, nor will I ever, acknowledge the right of a minority who happen to be a majority in a small part of our country, to opt out of our nation.

Deputies: Hear, hear.

An Taoiseach: I want to be as clear and as unequivocal as I can about that because suggestions have been made that I think to the contrary. But we have the factual situation that our country is partitioned and that one and a half million of our total population are outside the jurisdiction of this national parliament and that approximately two-thirds of that one and a half million at present want to remain outside the jurisdiction. I have said, and I recognise, that we cannot have a lasting and meaningful reunification of our country until we can persuade that majority that their place is with their fellow-countrymen in a united Ireland.

Perhaps I could at this stage refer to some remarks of Deputy Cosgrave in this context. He chose to sneer at the republicanism of the Fianna Fáil Party. But one thing is certain, and it is time the Fine Gael Deputies opposite were reminded of the fact — Fianna Fáil succeeded in making republicans of the lot of you—

Deputies: Hear, hear.

Mr P. Smith: They gave us stepping-stones but they would not walk on them.

An Taoiseach: — and you dare not ever again retreat from republicanism, as your predecessors did fifty years ago, because we will never let you.

I was really amazed to hear Deputy Cosgrave make the brazen claim that Fine Gael always had a consistent policy on partition. If Fine Gael or Cumann na nGaedheal or whatever one likes to call them were consistent, if they were firm, if they were strong, if they were truly republicans 50 years ago, there would not be any need now for the same kind of policy on partition that we have.

Mr Cosgrave: Was that the time you tossed the coin to see which side you would take?

An Taoiseach: That is an untruth.

Leas-Cheann Comhairle: The Taoiseach.

An Taoiseach: I will tell the story about that.

Mr L'Estrange: What about the Government of Ireland Act?

An Taoiseach: I never supported any political party but Fianna Fáil. One of my earliest recollections of a political party meeting was when Eamon de Valera came into Cork in 1932 and I carried a torch beside his carriage and I was only a young boy then. I will tell you what I did do. When I was first asked to stand, I did toss a coin as to whether I would or not stand for Fianna Fáil. That is the truth of that position.

An Taoiseach: Deputy Seán McBride, as he was then, approached me through a legal colleague in Cork to stand for his party and I completely rejected him. If you want to draw more of those facts out of me you are quite welcome.

Mr L'Estrange: What did Gerry Boland think of you?

Mr J. Lenehan: What did the German to whom the Deputy sold his land think of him?

A Deputy: An Egyptian.

But for anyone seeking suitable material for a black comedy which could be entitled, "Compliments Pass when the Quality Meet", a slow reading of these debates of 1970 would be very rewarding. Let us conclude with this slice of life from the midlands.

Mr O. J. Flanagan: Is it not true to say that law and order have broken down completely in the Republic? Is it not true to say that there is a law for the rich and a law for the poor? Is it not true to say that there is a legal law and a Taca law? Taca law is the law under which if you are a supporter of the Government your case is dismissed.

An Ceann Comhairle: That is a reflection on the judiciary.

Mr O.J. Flanagan: Oh, no. I meant the Department of Justice, not the judiciary. I want to make that very clear.

Mr Lalor: The Department of Justice does not dismiss cases.

Mr O.J. Flanagan: The Department of Justice deals with fines. I have known district justices to impose fines which were wiped out by the Department of Justice. I have known cases in which the rulings of the Attorney General were rather questionable and I honestly feel that the law is not administered as fairly as it might be.

Mr Lalor: The Deputy stated publicly that he wrote to a superintendent to quash convictions about cockfighting. The Deputy said that on television.

Mr O.J. Flanagan: I beg the Minister's pardon?

Mr Lalor: The Deputy said publicly that he wrote to the Garda authorities to quash cases in connection with illegal cockfighting.

Mr O.J. Flanagan: The Minister knows the circumstances under which cockfighting became illegal. It was during the Fenian times. The Fenians were making pikes and they used cockfighting as an excuse for the making of the pikes. In order to get at the Fenians a law was brought in which made cockfighting completely illegal.

Mr Lalor: So cockfighting is legal now, according to the Deputy.

Mr O. J. Flanagan: No, cockfighting is illegal.

An Ceann Comhairle: Let us get away from cockfighting.

Mr O.J. Flanagan: Cockfighting is illegal except when the cocks are within the Fianna Fáil Party when fighting is legal. Believe it or not, there are a good many cocks jumping very high at the moment.

The Republic settled down remarkably well after all that and addressed important issues like the negotiations to enter the EEC. Of course it continued to make the right noises after each atrocity in the Six Counties and the gradual dismantling of the apparatus of the northern state.

But the problem, such as it was, remained in its proper place. Reporters returning from duty across the Border were usually asked two questions when they arrived in Dublin: "Is it as bad as you say it is?" and "Any danger of the bloody thing spreading down here?"

In May 1972, the country entered the EEC: 83% of voters declaring in favour of the big battalions on a turnout of 71%. That was clear enough. Almost everyone was going to get something for nothing and we were now getting into the slip-stream of the most efficient countries in Europe and who could argue against that? It could do nothing but good for "that other problem up there" and, now that everyone would learn French and German, it would be the final excuse for ditching bloody Irish. Not even the Labour Party, although ideologically opposed to EEC membership (or so the tail that sought to wag the dog had decided), campaigned seriously against entry. The well-balanced television and radio programmes did little to balance the outcome. The lesson which was not learned for many years was that no matter how excellent the television programme, its impact is limited by the state of mind of the viewers: open, closed or idling in neutral.

The ideological left-wingers, who seemed to be masochistically opposed to free money for deserving rich and poor alike were reduced to trotting out the old Sinn Féin message of self-reliance and national pride. Some mentioned that it was high time the national wealth was redistributed. This smelt like another version of de Valera's "frugal comfort" and went down like a lead balloon with the classes who were making a fortune out of tearing down Dublin with one hand and buying Jack B. Yeats paintings to adorn their awful dwellings with the other.

It almost escaped notice here that Norway stayed out because of its fishing industry and that we struck a remarkably soft bargain when negotiating our fishing rights. The question nobody wished to ask was, "What have we got that Europe wants?" Too late it was realised

— if it was realised even then — that we had bartered our second greatest natural resource for the sake of bolstering up our first. Our potential "garden in the sea" had gone to join the "fourth green field" with scarcely a whinge to bid it goodbye.

The 70s, in case you had forgotten, were to be socialist. The Labour Party threw away its waiter's outfit and opened an eating-house of its own. Party leader Brendan "I am a Catholic first and an Irishman second" Corish, said that if the party betrayed its new-found backbone of independence, by deciding to partake in a coalition, he would resign from the leadership and decorate the backbenches. What he really meant was that he would have nothing against being Tánaiste and so it came to pass.

Others, too, saw the dawning of the day through the windows of their detached, red-brick, working-class houses in the suburbs. A posse of what the newspapers called "intellectuals and academics", with degrees like thermometers, broke into the Labour Party through the front door and the two-and-a-half party system was dead and gone. If ever there was a media revolution it was this.

In a speech of incredible pomposity Dr Cruise O'Brien, the biggest thermometer of them all and the most accurate naturally, announced that the votes of the under-thirties would free Ireland. The *Irish Times* was so excited by the good Doctor's speech in praise of his new-found Irish plaything that it handed Wolfe Tone and Armour of Ballymoney to its property experts for redevelopment and printed his speech in full. Despite the all-pervading pomposity it contains nuggets of exquisite irony. Take the younger generation, for instance:

> They know, as their parents' generation on the whole did not, that there are alternatives to unquestioning obedience to one's instructors, and to acquiescence in the *status quo* of one's environment. They also tend to share with those of the same age elsewhere their generation's impatience with the past, and with what

they regard as their elders' obsession with the past. They know little about the Irish Civil War of 1922, and its rights and wrongs leave them entirely cold. Because of the passage of time, the magic of Mr de Valera's name no longer reaches them, and can do nothing to transform the prosaic reality of the bourgeois politicians whom they now see ruling the country. The very names of our main parties — "Soldiers of Destiny" and "Kith and Kin of the Gael" — belong to a rhetoric which can only puzzle or amuse people of under thirty.

One can only advise the Doctor not to read that particular passage too loudly on the recently-scaled Hills of O'Zion in case the synagogue cat damages himself with a fit of laughing. However, shake this one three times before taking:

Many of these young people are coming into the Labour Party and they do so in the same spirit as animates their other activities: not because they approve of what their elders have done, but because they are confident of improving on it, through change. The young Sinn Féiners, in the early years of the century, were men and women of essentially the same type.

That was 1968 and the following year Jack Lynch called a general election and scuppered the Labour Party. He took off on a round of visits to convents in all parts of Ireland which had Oliver Flanagan holding on for dear life to his halo. Fianna Fáil ran a campaign of guilt by association, in tandem with Lynch's Holy Road-Show, which branded the new Labour Party as playing at the politics of greed, and Castro's Cuba and the nationalisation of land were more than hinted at. The smear worked and Fianna Fáil won an over-all majority of five.

Lemass and MacEntee, remembering past smears and Red scares, must have been proud of the reluctant, soft-spoken Taoiseach with eyes like a particularly reflective picture of the Sacred Heart. But the two old adversaries had by now found a new pastime outside politics: inflicting much more damage on the aspect of Ireland's finest street, in the interests of development and the creation of new jobs, than either gentleman succeeded in inflicting in 1916.

Despite the little bits of bother, particularly that Northern business that did not seem to be going away, the country was not doing badly at all. With almost no stenuous effort emigration, the greatest bulling sacred cow of them all, no longer existed. Every week the *Irish Post,* voice of the Irish in Britain, was full of advertisements for properties in Ireland and for the removal companies which would transport all you had back to booming Mary Horan's country. Many of those who returned had plundered the land of their temporary adoption to the point of no return and with taxmen snapping at their heels they came home to find out how soft a touch the auld sod was. They found the auld sod wide open. With the right connections you could site your pile of utterly vulgar concrete on a hairpin bend and get away with it.

The new Ireland was magic. The wild geese were returning. Instead of making television programmes about the wild and filthy Irishmen who crawled out of the walls surrounding Waterloo Station at night, waving bottles of meths and muttering, "Inivvergotofuggingmass, I fugging hate the fugging . . . giveusa butt", there was the clean-cut, total abstainer who had made "the few bob" and who was coming back, the Lord save us, to make a few more with his good Catholic wife and a dozen children.

Only the *Irish Post,* in its more non-profitmaking pages, cautioned that there might be more froth than porter in the glass the Emerald Isle was offering. But, in truth, everyone enjoyed some of the reflected glory of this emigration in reverse. It is hard to believe that it all happened about a decade ago and that already the rate of unemployment is approaching twenty per cent of the work-force; despite the return of the secret emigration which not even RTE has got around to acknowledging.

In February 1973, having presided over Ireland's entry into the EEC and let Dessie O'Malley loose on the Provos, Lynch called a de Valera-style election. The unspoken reason was that the under-eighteens would have the vote in April and they were more than likely to vote for the Labour Party's socialism, having re-read the O'Brien script and the pamphlet with the unfortunate title, "Corish Speaks". However, the electorate decided that this was to be a "Put Them Out" election and the Labour Party deserted socialism without ever having defined their particular version of it. God smiled on them too and they entered into a Coalition with Fine Gael. There was nothing new, pussy cat!

Things went well in the beginning. Edward Heath decided to bang some heads together in Sunningdale and the Power-Sharing Executive emerged. It is reported that Cosgrave actually spoke during the negotiations, a happening which cheered Heath considerably as he was beginning to worry about the Taoiseach's brooding silences. When the Executive collapsed the Dublin Government decided on a new policy. The central problem was not partition but IRA violence so they set up a Heavy Gang of Gardaí Neamhshíochánta to kick the fear of God into, and many confessions out of, all suspects.

Having found in the charismatic figure of Paddy Cooney a worthy successor to Kevin O'Higgins Cosgrave sought and found someone who was cut out to run a Pro-Partition campaign. As Dr O'Brien had spent some of his formative years running an Anti-Partition campaign he took to the new job with such an appetite that he kept it up as a hobby for years after he retired from politics. The central issue in the new campaign was that anyone who favoured a united Ireland, or who maintained that such an outcome to the national problem was a valid political position, was a Provo-supporter if not the real McCoy. Even poor nice Jack Lynch's attitude was described by the crusading Doctor as "Puss-in-Boots Provoism".

Then things began to go seriously wrong. The Taoiseach

voted against his own proposed legislation on contraception. When Minister Cooney's attention was drawn to his Taoiseach's presence in the wrong starting-stall in the Dáil, he is said to have uttered a very bad word.

The Taoiseach was accompanied by his beloved disciple Dick Burke, who had put himself in the running for the post-Cosgrave party leadership. He told inquiring journalists that unlike Garret FitzGerald he understood the Ireland that lay beyond the Dead Man Murray's. The difference between them was that Garret had never jumped over a ditch in Munster, done his "wee jobbie" and then wiped himself with a dock-leaf: a story calculated to bring horror to the hearts of the makers of scented toilet-paper.

They caused the President to resign. To the surprise of those who continued to take liberal politicians as seriously as they seemed to take their principles, the Garrets, the Justins, the Conors and the rest of them in Cabinet seemed to sit on their hands and concentrate their minds on their pensions. The high standards they laid down for others were certainly not for them.

This unique happening in Irish politics was brought about by the untimely death of Erskine Childers who, to the surprise of everyone, particularly T.F. O'Higgins the Fine Gael candidate, won the presidential election of 1973. In 1966, against de Valera O'Higgins thought he could not win and almost did; in 1973 he thought he could not lose and did.

Cosgrave was very put out that Childers had to go off and die on him while seemingly in the whole of his health. Cosgrave did not want a presidential election, but neither did he want some Fianna Fáil miscreant visited on him. He called in the best English-speaker in the Cabinet, gave him an Irish-speaking mate and sent them both down town to float "The Widda's" name as an agreed candidate. The balloon came to grief on Wolfe Tone's big toe in D'Olier Street. Cosgrave had to accept Cearbhall O Dálagih reluctantly and he tore strips off his chief communicator while his mate fled to a remote Gaeltacht where he runs a small but exclusive business.

Cosgrave's worst fears were realised when President O Dálaigh began to behave like a liberal lawyer and referred the Emergency Powers Bill to the Supreme Court. Like a good master of hounds the Taoiseach isolated this mongrel fox and one of his favourites — bluff, gypsy-loving Minister for Defence, Paddy Donegan — fixed the President good and proper. In a military establishment in Mullingar he referred to the actions of O Dálaigh with the Bill as the work of "a thundering idiot and a fucking disgrace"; an utterence which official reticence, amazing for such liberated times, has bowdlerised.

It would be wrong to imagine that Cosgrave's motive was to chase O Dálaigh out of the Park. He did not possess the imagination for such deviousness. He merely wanted to inform the President, at one remove, that he was not performing his tasks in a helpful way. He was the most surprised man in Ireland when O Dálaigh walked out. He could not understand why O Dálaigh would not accept Donegan's much-proffered apology ("Yerra, you know how it is, Karl auld stock! No hard feelings and all that!") and insisted that it was a matter for a Taoiseach who had not said one word. Men just did not walk out of good jobs for some sort of foothery principle! Look at his cabinet of high-principled legal and academic luminaries ...

Even the political correspondents refused to believe that any Government could be as unpopular as the Coalition had become when the 1977 election came about. Even without the Dutch auction to end all Dutch auctions Fianna Fáil would have won by a margin which would have made Jack Lynch's life more comfortable in his pooltical middle-age, and without plunging the country up to its ear-holes in debt.

And this is more or less where we have chosen to get out. What has happened since is common knowledge and of little real political import. The exception is the North. The shadow of the troubles has now settled heavily over the

Republic and cannot be willed away. Even the most myopic realise that there is no possible hope of disengagement for anyone on the island; something which does not apply to Britain.

Apart from that the country seems to have settled down to contemplating its navel with deepening disgust and consequent depression. We have become exceedingly sorry for ourselves. Our expectations were raised high but not realised and now we want to know who went wrong, where and why?

All through the island, when the marrow has been sucked out of the bones of the latest scandal, a great wailing can be heard. "Let's face it," they cry, "This country is finished. There is no hope, no future; just bigger tax bills and a black economy. Where, oh where did we go wrong?"

We have already quoted Seán Lemass on his view of patriotism. Unfortunately, he did not tell us how the spirit he regarded as a necessary vehicle for this practical patriotism could be revived when times were bad. But he once referred to what he regarded as a national weakness, during a Dáil debate in 1960: "I am not at all sure that the main weakness in the Irish character, if there is any weakness at all, is an undue disposition to be sorry for ourselves. I personally hold the philosophy, which I think applies to nations as well as to individuals, that once you start getting sorry for yourself, you are finished."

Lemass was of an age to know that out of seemingly barren soil grew the great movements which fostered national pride and self-respect and led to the gaining of that freedom which was supposed to lead to even fuller freedom: the GAA, the Gaelic League, the Abbey Theatre, the ITGWU, the Volunteers, Sinn Féin, the Co-Operative Movement and the IRA. Readers will come to their own conclusions concerning the present state of those organisations which survive. For light relief they may also cast an eye on some of our present-day political thinkers: those who counsel "Whatever you do, do nothing" on the

North when such inaction is clearly impossible now, or those who try to convince you that Uncle Mick who joined the IRA and was firing into the RIC Barracks was no more of the Irish patriot than Uncle Joe who was inside the barracks firing back.

At least, sad and all as the country has become, those disposed to regard a joke as a serious matter will never be short of a laugh.

13

Where there's no will
there's no way

It is appropriate that a survey such as this, which asks many questions without providing any answers or holding out any hope of improvement in our affairs, should be made up of an odd number of chapters: a number regarded as lucky by some and unlucky by others, just like the national colour. However, green is also the colour of the world's most powerful currency unit and as Patrick Kavanagh once said, "Money talks everywhere but only money seems to talk in Ireland." Naturally: we are, after all a very spiritual people with a spiritual empire stretching from Zambia to the itinerant settlement in Tallaght, if it still exists at the time of publication.

It is now time to face hard facts. At some time in the not too distant future you will be called on to vote in a general election. Since Fianna Fáil's Great Rate Robbery of 1977 we have had a series of "Put Them Out", "Put Them In" elections. In most of them, apart from the Hunger Strike election, minor scandals, gossip and questions of personality seemed to shoulder serious questions off the stage. This is one reason, dear reader, why the present crisis was half-way up the leg of your trousers before you really knew about it.

Readers of the works of Mr James Joyce will find the present situation in Ireland curiously reminiscent of the political scene in Dublin at the turn of the century, as portrayed in many of his works.

RTE must take its share of the blame for this preoccupation with the trivia of politics: a true Trivial Pursuit which it failed to patent. Many political writers must take the blame (something they are not particularly good about doing) for getting personally involved in a bogus moral crusade which was little more than dressing up petty political gossip. They should attach the following words of H.L. Mencken to the tops of their typewriters: "The worst government is the most moral. One composed of cynics is often very tolerant and humane. But when fanatics are on top there is no limit to oppression." Indeed, as if we did not have it in our own house! However, Mencken was taking competence for granted when he wrote that and it would be a great fool who would take competence in an Irish politician for granted.

RTE made many excellent political programmes but it also established a practice, during election campaigns, of dissecting voting patterns in the most obscure corners of Ireland and making them central to nothing on earth apart from themselves. It was an exercise calculated to enable Ted Nealon, its founder, to display his fascination with the Junior Football, "C" Division, School of Political Jersey-pulling. Those seeking in vain for some reason for Mr Nealon's appointment to what passes for a Ministry for Culture should keep this in mind and reach for their whistles instead of pulling their guns.

How the people of Attythomaisreevy are going to vote and where their votes are going to "travel" become all-important in this type of spurious analysis. Indeed, all other issues are banished, apart from the weird political faction-fighting in which the people of this awful place, and their ancestors back to the times of O'Connell, were involved. It would be against the rules to mention that the place has a sixty per cent rate of emigration and that those who stay are on the dole. It would be ill-mannered to recount that it is said that when a bull is seen mounting a cow in Attythomaisreevy he may not be seeking that "violent spasm of pleasure" but merely wanting to find out if there is a bit of grass in any of the nearby fields. The question to ask, naturally, is "should Attythomaisreevy exist at all and how can it be done away with painlessly?"

Gay Byrne, father confessor to the Irish nation, has raised the question of Ireland's future on numerous occasions. He seems to lay a lot of blame for current problems on the shoulders of what he terms "begrudgers", therefore he may not take kindly to our own little stab at analysis. He may have a different species of begrudger in mind and that is understandable.

During his recent much-publicised financial troubles it is quite probable that for every citizen who was heard to say, "Terrible thing that about poor Gay, after all his hard work", he heard of ten who said, "Good enough for the stingy hoor! Wouldn't spend Christmas I believe. Must have his shaggin' communion money." Such begrudgers are beyond our ken and beneath our contempt if we did ken them. And to prove our point we are going to allow ourselves to make a suggestion.

Why does Gay Byrne not take the *Late Late Show* to Iceland and come to his vast audience live from Reykjavik?

We are not joking. Here is a country with scarcely any interior, no railways because of that, only four months' growth on what arable land there is and almost entirely dependent on fishing and fish-based industries for survival. Like ourselves the country suffered heavy emigration between 1900 and 1960 but now has a population of 240,000 with a standard of living equal to Denmark's. The country has no army but one of the highest standards of public health in the world. Its small fleet of fishery-protection vessels fought and won a serious fishing limits war with Britain in the mid-70s: dubbed the Cod War by Fleet Street to take the sting out of it.

Almost all education to university level is free, there is no illiteracy and as well as a radio and television service (and a feature film industry in their own language) the country supports five daily papers, seven national weeklies, twenty-four monthlies and fifty publishing houses. If Gay Byrne does go there he will be particularly interested, one would guess, in the country's five trades unions. We out-gun them there with about 50.

Iceland has the world's first popularly elected female head of state, Vigdís Finnbogadóttir, who also happens to be a single parent. The economy is a mixture of private and state enterprise and is really too heavily dependent on fishing.

Having mentioned the Icelandic language this is as good a place as any to take a quick look at that scrub bull, masquerading as a sacred cow, the Irish language. It is often said that we have made a total mess of its revival and while that is true the mess is no worse than any of the other national messes one wishes to contemplate. In a recent Thomas Davis Lecture, Professor Joe Lee from UCC raised some interesting points which Icelanders would probably find amusing, if not strange.

He said that we are unique among the states of Europe in having abandoned our language "reputedly to sell the cow". "The irony is that other small states, who lack the imagination to take so apparently progressive a step as abandoning their obscure language, have sold the cow distinctly more successfully than ourselves. We bartered the language, but we couldn't even get a proper price for it. The language is lost unless Government fosters its revival through example and this is unlikely to happen. The language will therefore remain a museum piece, to be fleetingly and furtively exhibited on occasions of public ritual, a ghostly reminder of our unusual feat of losing on the swings and losing on the roundabouts."

A recent example of the ritualistic use of Irish, by one not noted for his devotion to its use, was Garret Fitzgerald's use of it when he spoke at Hillsborough Castle. As far as could be ascertained it was a way of bringing the SDLP and the Dublin Government to windward of Sinn Féin and "Tiocfaidh ár lá". Be that as it may it was as interesting a public display of political schizophrenia as was seen in Ireland since Daniel O'Connell addressed a meeting in

Clifden in 1843 and Eamon de Valera addressed another there about a century later. O'Connell spoke English and hardly anyone understood him; de Valera spoke Irish and hardly anyone understood him either. Small wonder that schizophrenia is top of the loonie pops in Ireland, particularly west of the Shannon.

Maybe Gay should also go to Switzerland and find out how people succeeded in finding a way to live in peace and harmony, not through the melting-pot theory (Uncle Mick and Uncle Joe as different aspects of freedom-fighting) but through maintaining cultural, religious and linguistic differences .... but on second thoughts perhaps we should withdraw these suggestions. At best the programmes would be met with a sigh of indifference; at worst they might lead to a self-fulfilling and utterly useless Great National Debate. It is utterly useless because it ends not in action but in boredom: "Let's face it, what have we to learn from a bunch of smelly fishermen. Fine thing that President though .... wonder who the lucky mystery man was?".

One of the most important books published in Ireland for years is Frank McDonald's *The Destruction of Dublin*. It is also one of the most truly shocking as it describes in meticulous detail what our own "gentry", in the persons of our property developers and other land sharks, did to Dublin; not that the rest of the country is any better and is even likely to be much worse in time.

But the really shocking thing about the book is that although it did give rise to a debate, on television and in the press, it is likely to have no practical effect. That is no fault of the author's, nor of anyone else but those who refuse to adopt civilised attitudes towards preserving what is part of the country's wealth, as well as its heritage.

It could be, of course, that the property developer is fairly representative of what our own gentry turned out to be. In which case the blacksmith in West Cork was truly a prophet without honour.

Even a begrudger can feel shame. The thought of being

ruled by a confraternity of goms, the majority of whom should never have been "let out", is a sobering one; the fact that they are freely elected by people vastly more intelligent than themselves is shattering. For it must be admitted that we are better than that when given a chance; even half a chance ....

When Mark Twain wrote a pamphlet in 1899, "Concerning the Jews", he berated that race for failing to organise themselves politically in countries where they had acquired some wealth:

> With all his splendid capacities and all his fat wealth he is not today politically important in any country. In America, as early as 1854, the ignorant Irish hod-carrier, who had a spirit of his own and a way of exposing it to the weather, made it apparent to all that he must be politically reckoned with; yet fifteen years before that we hardly knew what an Irishman looked like. As an intelligent force, and numerically, he has always been away down, but he has governed the country just the same. It was because he was *organised*. It made his vote valuable — in fact, essential.

An Irish joke may be a far more serious thing than even most Irish people realise. Like the Jews and some of the central European peoples — particularly the Poles — we often express outselves most clearly in relation to our problems in this form.

The hotel porter, to take a basic example of what is regarded as witlessness, who says he cannot put the guest's telegram under the bedroom door because it is on a tray is merely indicating in an oblique way that he expects a tip. The man who scratches his head at the side of the road, when the motorist asks for directions to get to Mullingar, and says, "Jasus, if I was going to Mullingar I wouldn't start from here at all", is saying that an error of planning has rendered a comparatively easy journey unnecessarily complicated.

That is as far as we can go along a road which would be easily paved with good suggestions, but there is no general plan and even if a plan existed it is doubtful if the will to implement it could be found. To that extent the country is bankrupt; a more serious form of bankruptcy than any financial swamp you can image, in or out of your dreams.

And there we must leave you to answer the door to the knocks of Garret's men, Charlie's men, Dick's men, Dessie's men and the men with the ideology and the non-existent army. Ideally, the Workers Party should be able to exploit the present difficulties politically on a national scale. For its own singular reasons it has chosen to advance slowly, adopting a lot of post-Fenian cloak-and-dagger rituals and semi-communistic sacramentals, even in matters of recruitment of members.

As to the nonexistent army which drives the party leaders to the brink of mental breakdown it would be as well for them to come clean and be done with it. What became of the arms the Official IRA had when they were dumped? The answer to that, which any helpful member of the Special Branch will supply, is that they are retained for possible use in the event of attack by the brutal, bloody and politically bankrupt Provos. In that case would it be correct to surmise, comrade, that there are comrades who are trained to use them, if and when the time comes, and that these comrades would be acting under orders of superiors who would be responsible to what one might term an Army Council?

No! No! Of course not, this is a nasty Provo smear! To which the only possible reply is, "My arse in parsley".

The Labour Party seems to be heading for one of its periodic baptisms by immersion in Socialism, with Michael D. Higgins giving one of his brilliant imitations of an Italian opera star doing an impression of an old-fashioned Redemptorist preacher. After Michael O'Leary's solo-attempt to prove that there was no difference between Labour and Fine Gael one hesitates before making any predictions about the party leadership. We understand that young Mrs Spring enjoys being the "Tanaistee's" wife but other straws in the wind indicate that what's left of the 80s may well be Socialist. . . . and about time too!

That looks like making it safe for Charlie and the collection of over-dressed bookies' runners that form his entourage. God between us and all harm, and the present crowd look as if they would make a mess of a Referendum on giving away Free Fivers (no offence to the Workers Party intended), but will you look at what will replace them? If Charlie wins it will be his last hurrah and then there will be another succession race; there will be one much earlier if he loses. . . .

A Fianna Fail win would suit the element in Fine Gael who realise that there is a limit to what national handlers can do for poor old Garret. His popularity with the English press is no substitute for the parcel of votes in Attythomaisreevy which are needed to save the last seat, regardless of the fact that most of the voters are cracked. Garret must go, Fine Gael must regroup in opposition, mark Fianna Fáil until they part at the seams and return with an over-all majority while Labour can play "Wee Willie Pinkie" to their hearts' content.

That is the thinking and Bruton from the Plains of Meath is the man to carry it out, with Barry the teaman caught for pace on the run in. . . . one could go on, and on, and on, and you can bet your life that many an expert will, but the point of it all is much simpler, more straight-forward, and infinitely more important. Let's face it and be clear about it. . . .

THE REAL POINT IS THAT ALL THIS DOESN'T MATTER
A FIDDLER'S FART ON THE CLIFFS OF MOHER
TO THE COUNTRY'S REAL PROBLEMS.

And that is probably the one completely accurate and true statement in the entire book. It is enough . . . . to make one think. . . . when those knocks come to the door. . . .